"*The Family Bible Devotional* is an extension of Sarah's passion as a Christ follower and the commitment she has to pass on her love of Christ to her children. I am excited about this new volume, as it focuses us on the life and ministry of Jesus. What an incredible resource for us all, as we seek to love God with all our hearts and love others as we love ourselves!"

DR. STEVEN COLE, executive director, The Brethren Church Denomination

"Do you long for your kids to have a knowledge and a love for God's Word but are unsure of how to help this happen in a natural, fun, and winsome way? This devotional is for you. The layout encourages questions, provides activities, and enables both parents and children to grow together in a deeper understanding of God's love for each one of us."

SUSAN ALEXANDER YATES, bestselling author, speaker, and blogger

"There is something for everyone in this delightful way to build the foundations of faith with your family! The flexibility of the lessons and approachability of the activities allow for everyone to participate."

BILL LUDWIG, lead pastor, Five Stones Community Church

Praise for the Volume 1

The Family Bible Devotional: Stories from the Bible to Help Kids & Parents Engage & Love Scripture

"When it comes to reading the Bible with my kids, I am among the well-meaning and terrified. I find that I don't know where to start or how to navigate past my own faith baggage to engage my kids in healthy, wonder-filled conversations about God's story. This Bible devotional offers a way in. It honors questions, engages creativity, and is flexible enough to work for your particular family, no matter where you're at. What a gift!"

ADDIE ZIERMAN, author of *When We Were on Fire* and *Night Driving*

T0051420

"*The Family Bible Devotional* is a great resource for parents who want to engage their children in fresh and meaningful discussions about the Bible as they explore stories and passages together. Fun activities, interesting facts, and thought-provoking questions will turn family devotions from boring to exciting. I wish I had this book when my kids were growing up!"

CRYSTAL BOWMAN, best-selling, award-winning author of over 100 books for children, including *Our Daily Bread for Kids*

"*The Family Bible Devotional* has added a fresh new dimension to mornings with my 13-year-old daughter. Background information, Scripture unhampered by verse notations (it reads like a story!), and thought-provoking questions and prayer prompts not only serve to structure our discussions during busy breakfast time, but challenge us to consider Scripture from new perspectives. My daughter has been inspired to ask tough questions and deepen her understanding of the Bible, all before the school bus comes around the corner!"

TANIA RUNYAN, poet and author

"In this excellent devotional, Sarah Wells has packed a lifetime of inspiration and joyful applications that will guide families into a deeper appreciation of Scripture."

DANDI DALEY MACKALL, award-winning author of over 500 books for adults and children

"When writing for children, especially when topics are confusing or tough to wade through, I think it's important for kids to have a narrator they can trust, and Wells doesn't disappoint. Her writing is friendly and thought-provoking, and the activities she's designed to go along with the devotions are creative and fun. Here's a family devotional that allows parents to walk alongside their children as they explore God's story, and find their place in it."

CALLIE FEYEN, author of *Romeo & Juliet: The Teacher Diaries*

"I like it a lot!"

ROSIE, age 9, who kept reading the book on her own after family devotions were done

The
FAMILY BIBLE
DEVOTIONAL

STORIES FROM THE GOSPELS
TO HELP KIDS & PARENTS
LOVE GOD & LOVE OTHERS

SARAH M. WELLS

Our Daily Bread
Publishing™

Published in association with Books & Such Literary Management, 52 Mission Circle, Suite 122, PMB 170, Santa Rosa, CA 95409-5370, www.booksandsuch.com.

Library of Congress Cataloging-in-Publication Data

Names: Wells, Sarah M., author.
Title: The family bible devotional : stories from the gospels to help kids
   and parents love God and love others / Sarah M. Wells.
Description: Grand Rapids : Our Daily Bread Publishing, 2022. | Summary:
   "Experience the power of God's love as a family"-- Provided by
   publisher.
Identifiers: LCCN 2021047112 | ISBN 9781640701380 (paperback)
Subjects: LCSH: Bible stories, English. | Bible--Miscellanea. |
   Families--Religious life.
Classification: LCC BS550.3 .W455 2022 | DDC 220.95/05--dc23
LC record available at https://lccn.loc.gov/2021047112

Printed in the United States of America
22 23 24 25 26 27 28 29 / 8 7 6 5 4 3 2 1

Contents

Introduction

The first volume of *The Family Bible Devotional* aimed to provide families with a hearty foundation of Old Testament stories interwoven with stories about Jesus. This structure was intentional; Jesus lived, taught, ministered, died, and rose again within the context of a Jewish world that was extremely well versed in their Scriptures (the Christian's Old Testament). As Christians, we live and breathe through the Living Word, Jesus Christ, who as the Son of God is our representative of God the Father. Jesus said, "I and the Father are one" (John 10:30 NIV). If we want to know who God is, we look to Jesus. When we read the Old Testament as Christians, we ought to read it through the lens of what we know to be true about Jesus.

Whereas the first volume strove to build a foundation of knowledge and faith in who God is, this second volume of *The Family Bible Devotional* examines how the Lord interacted with people. Jesus said in Matthew 22:37–39 that the greatest commandment is to love the Lord your God, "and the second is like it: 'Love your neighbor as yourself'" (NIV).

This age isn't so different from any other: People still seek power over other people. People still pursue pleasure at the expense of others. People still value profit over relationships. The universal message of Christ—to love God and love your neighbor—is just as relevant and critical to our health as humans as it has been at any other time in history. As parents or guardians, we have the responsibility and privilege to instill the love of Christ in our children, thereby putting in the good work necessary to usher in the kingdom of heaven on earth.

The stories we read and study together in this devotional will help us see how the Lord of the universe demonstrated his love for us: he laid down his life, and he modeled a life of loving God and loving his neighbors. In this time of division, us-versus-them debates, and disillusionment, we can learn so much from Jesus's interactions with his disciples to shape and guide the way we love one another.

What does a "one another" love rooted in Christ look like? This is what we'll discover and practice together with your family throughout this devotional. I am elated to join you on this journey with Christ—the Living Word of God—as the Holy Spirit reveals to us how God loves the world, and what it means for us to go and do likewise. Perhaps by doing so, we will indeed bring heaven to earth.

Blessings on this season of your journey with God! May God bring you and your family ever closer to each other, and to completion, until the day of Christ Jesus (Philippians 1:6).

Guide to Using This Devotional

If you are familiar with the first volume of *The Family Bible Devotional*, you will see that the structure of the devotional entries remains the same. Each devotional begins with an introductory paragraph to set the scene, followed by the Bible story. Some guiding questions are provided for your family to consider, along with a pivotal question: Is there anything that confuses you? Sometimes the Bible can be confusing, so this question provides your family members the opportunity to be honest and vulnerable along their journeys with God. We do not have all of the answers, and that is okay. Faith is about trusting the Lord, even and especially when we don't have a full understanding. God is worthy of our trust.

Following the questions, there is a short reflection to guide your understanding of the story of the day. A brief prayer prompt is designed to help your family talk to God. Activities to reinforce your reading of the Scripture are provided. Finally, some historical background information or a fun fact related to the story ends the devotional entry.

While the first *Family Bible Devotional* toggled back and forth between Old and New Testament stories, this second volume focuses on the Gospels (Matthew, Mark, Luke, and John), which are collections of stories about Jesus's life and ministry. The devotionals are not organized chronologically; instead, they are grouped together by the types of relationships Jesus had with his closest disciples, women, people who had different views of God or no beliefs whatsoever, his friends, his family members, and even his enemies.

HOW TO READ THE DEVOTIONAL

While the devotional was written in the order you see here, if you find yourself drawn to a particular theme, no one is telling you to read it from beginning to end. The introductions to each entry provide enough context to be read individually, so if you are not reading through from start to finish, the story, reflections, and activities should be able to stand alone.

If your family is like mine, our lives ebb and flow in terms of busy seasons and quieter seasons. There are times when sitting down together for a meal (which is when we practiced most of these devotionals) is rare, and other times when we gather as a family every night. Dinnertime seems to be the most consistent space for us to gather together, but if a morning devotional or pre-bedtime routine works best for you, go with that! If the whole family can't be together, work through a devotional time with just one child, or some of your family, and consider that to be a blessed season you get to share with that member of your family.

Don't beat yourself up if you get out of a rhythm—our best intentions are often thwarted by work, school, health issues, family crises, and more. Remember: Our journeys with Christ are lifelong. God will meet us in our busyness and our quiet if we invite the Holy Spirit into those seasons.

That being said, if you love structure and guidelines to help you stay disciplined, there are fifty-two entries included in this devotional, so if you want to read weekly, you can make your way through this devotional in one year.

ABOUT HARD STORIES AND QUESTIONS

Life is filled with a lot of hard subjects that can sometimes be difficult to talk about. One of the gifts of Scripture is that God does not shy away from hard topics; after all, our Savior was crucified on a cross! Some of the stories we read together can prompt conversation about subjects in your family's life that might be sensitive or challenging. Lean into those moments and let your children process those hard topics together with you.

There's no doubt that your children are going to experience hard things; Jesus promised it. But God has given you each other to weather those questions, doubts, worries, and sufferings together. It's okay not to know the answers to their questions. It's okay to admit this. It shows your children that you can have questions about God's mysteries and still trust him fully, because God has proven himself to be trustworthy.

ABOUT TRANSLATIONS

In the book of Genesis, God speaks creation into existence. In the book of John, God is called the Word. It is through language that humankind discovers and ascribes meaning to the world.

We live in an age of many languages. We are two millennia removed from Christ and the original languages of the New Testament, which was primarily written in Greek. The writers of the Gospels likely referenced a source text that was composed in Aramaic. The Old Testament was written in Hebrew. It was an entire fifteen hundred years after Christ before the New Testament was first translated into English. As of the writing of this book, the Bible has been translated into 704 languages,[1] and there have been around 900 English translations or paraphrases of the Bible (some complete and others incomplete).[2]

With that long history of translation and interpretation behind us, I've chosen to reference just three translations of the Bible, rotating between them to provide families with a taste of the variety of styles and rich texture of meaning revealed through different Bible versions. If you are particularly fond of one translation over others, feel free to read that translation alongside or in place of the translations I've chosen. God's Word transcends translation.

ABOUT THE ACTIVITIES

I wrote in the first volume of the devotional that you should feel free to skip around and do what is best for the attention span and maturity of your family members, but that you should try your best not to skip the activities. This is where the rubber meets the road, where faith meets action, where knowing becomes doing. While many of these activities are lighthearted and fun, they are also intended to help your family practice the spiritual disciplines that invite Christ into your daily lives.

If you are unfamiliar with spiritual disciplines, I encourage you to explore the many ways God invites us to connect with the Trinity in order to grow in grace and truth, for our own sake and for the sake of our children. To help come up with some of the activities in this devotional, I referenced *Spiritual Disciplines Handbook: Practices That Transform Us* by Adele Ahlberg Calhoun. Another influential book that can help you understand and grow through spiritual disciplines is Richard J. Foster's *Celebration of Discipline: The Path to Spiritual Growth.*

Section 1

UNLIKELY DISCIPLES

Bringing Together the Band of Disciples

SETTING UP THE STORY

Every friendship has a beginning. There was a time before you met your best friend, and then there's everything after. Today we will read about the first time four of Jesus's disciples met Jesus and how their relationships began. *Disciple* is another word for a student—you'll see this word a lot throughout the gospel stories about Jesus. As you read today's story, think about how each of Jesus's disciples meets him and what makes them follow him.

READ: JOHN 1:35–51 (NIV)

The next day John was there again with two of his disciples. When he saw Jesus passing by, he said, "Look, the Lamb of God!"

When the two disciples heard him say this, they followed Jesus. Turning around, Jesus saw them following and asked, "What do you want?"

They said, "Rabbi" (which means "Teacher"), "where are you staying?"

"Come," he replied, "and you will see."

So they went and saw where he was staying, and they spent that day with him. It was about four in the afternoon.

Andrew, Simon Peter's brother, was one of the two who heard what John had said and who had followed Jesus. The first thing Andrew did was to find his brother Simon and tell him, "We have found the Messiah" (that is, the Christ). And he brought him to Jesus.

Jesus looked at him and said, "You are Simon son of John. You will be called Cephas" (which, when translated, is Peter).

The next day Jesus decided to leave for Galilee. Finding Philip, he said to him, "Follow me."

Philip, like Andrew and Peter, was from the town of Bethsaida. Philip found Nathanael and told him, "We have found the one Moses wrote about in the Law, and about whom the prophets also wrote—Jesus of Nazareth, the son of Joseph."

"Nazareth! Can anything good come from there?" Nathanael asked.

"Come and see," said Philip.

When Jesus saw Nathanael approaching, he said of him, "Here truly is an Israelite in whom there is no deceit."

"How do you know me?" Nathanael asked.

Jesus answered, "I saw you while you were still under the fig tree before Philip called you."

Then Nathanael declared, "Rabbi, you are the Son of God; you are the king of Israel."

Jesus said, "You believe because I told you I saw you under the fig tree. You will see greater things than that." He then added, "Very truly I tell you, you will see 'heaven open, and the angels of God ascending and descending on' the Son of Man."

TALK ABOUT IT

- How does Jesus meet each of the disciples in today's story?
- How did you meet one of your best friends?
- What did you have in common with them that helped you become friends?
- What is Nathanael's reaction when Philip tells him about Jesus?
- Have you ever made assumptions about a person only later to become friends? How did your opinion of them change?

Parents: During each family devotional, there will be the opportunity for asking questions—the parents get to ask questions, and the kids get to ask questions too. If you don't know the answer, it's okay to say so. As parents, we can empower our children to ask questions about God and the Bible. This curiosity and freedom will pave the way for a meaningful and healthy relationship with God as they grow into adults. Be willing to share your own questions about God or that day's story during this time. Sharing our own journeys of faith with our kids will help them see how you can have doubts and fears and still love God and be loved by God.

- Is there anything that confuses you about this first story? If so, it's okay! Let's talk about it.
- Do you have any questions about John 1:35–51?

CLOSING THOUGHT

Most of the people we read about today met Jesus through someone else: John the Baptist and Jesus were cousins. Andrew met Jesus through John the Baptist. Simon Peter met him through his brother, Andrew. Nathanael met him through his friend, Philip. Jesus was (and is) always in our world, but sometimes it takes a friend or family member to show him to us in order for us to see him.

Every person who meets Jesus has a story of how their lives were different before they met him and what their lives are like after. We know from Luke 5 that Simon Peter and his brother, Andrew, used to be fishermen, but after Jesus invited them to follow him, he said, "Don't be afraid; from now on you will fish for people" (Luke 5:10 NIV).

When Nathanael learned where Jesus was from, his immediate reaction was doubt—*can anything good come from there?!* But upon meeting Jesus, his opinion of him changed immediately, and Nathanael decided to follow him.

No matter how we meet Jesus or what opinions we have about him, God's love has the power to change our lives.

PRAYER PROMPT

Whether you learned about God from a parent, a family member, a friend, or a stranger, let's thank God today for that person and pray for the courage and faith to share the good news of God's love with the people in our lives.

ACTIVITY #1: PHONE A FRIEND

Is there a person in your life whose faith in God you admire? Ask them to share their story about how they came to know Jesus. When we hear other people's stories about how Jesus has changed their lives, it encourages us in our own faith journey.

ACTIVITY #2: THANKS, PAL!

Think about someone who has shown you God's love and helped you to know God better. Have you ever told them? Draw or write a thank you note to that person for bringing you closer to Jesus.

Four Gospels, Same Jesus

Matthew, Mark, Luke, and John are the four books of the Bible that tell the good news, or "gospel," about Jesus. Each of the authors of these books wrote about Jesus for specific readers. They come to the story of Jesus with various backgrounds and purposes, so sometimes the stories are told differently. The differences can be confusing.

Imagine you're at a birthday party for a friend. Your friend's brother, parents, and other friends from school are there. Later on, when everyone talks about that party, they retell what happened from their perspective. Each story is a little different but helps you to see your friend through others' eyes. The same is true of the Gospels—sometimes the stories are similar and sometimes they are different, but all of them together help us to know Jesus better.

Partying with the New Apostle

SETTING UP THE STORY

Simon Peter, Andrew, Philip, and Nathanael were introduced to Jesus and became his disciples through connections with family and friends. As we study more of Jesus's friends, family, and followers, we'll find that Jesus's closest disciples came from all kinds of backgrounds. Jesus and his community were Jewish and very familiar with their religion. Just like today, there were a lot of opinions about what it meant to follow God, even among those who practiced the same religion. In today's passage, Jesus invites Levi, an unlikely character, into his ministry.

READ: LUKE 5:27–32 (MSG)

After this he went out and saw a man named Levi at his work collecting taxes. Jesus said, "Come along with me." And he did—walked away from everything and went with him.

Levi gave a large dinner at his home for Jesus. Everybody was there, tax men and other disreputable characters as guests at the dinner. The Pharisees and their religion scholars came to his disciples greatly offended. "What is he doing eating and drinking with misfits and 'sinners'?"

Jesus heard about it and spoke up, "Who needs a doctor: the healthy or the sick? I'm here inviting outsiders, not insiders—an invitation to a changed life, changed inside and out."

TALK ABOUT IT

- Why do you think Jesus was at Levi's party?
- Why do you think the Pharisees and religious people were offended about the party?
- What do you think Jesus meant when he told the Pharisees that he's here to invite the outsiders, not the insiders?

- Who do you think Jesus would spend time with today, based on the story we just read?
- Is there anything that confuses you about this story? If so, it's okay! Let's talk about it.
- Do you have any questions about Luke 5:27–32?

CLOSING THOUGHT

You can probably tell from today's story that Levi wasn't the religious folks' type. The Pharisees weren't happy about the kinds of people Jesus hung out with, and they often disagreed with what Jesus said and did too. We'll see their frustration with Jesus often in our stories.

The Pharisees weren't bad people. They were the keepers of the law and the ones who studied Scripture, trying their hardest to please God. They sincerely wanted to do what was right, and they thought they were doing a pretty good job. They certainly thought they were better than the "sinners" like Levi. When they saw Jesus being friends with people who weren't even trying to do the right thing, they assumed that Jesus didn't care about God's laws as much as they did. But Jesus told his followers that he cared a lot: "Don't suppose for a minute that I have come to demolish the Scriptures—either God's Law or the Prophets. I'm not here to demolish but to complete. I am going to put it all together" (Matthew 5:17 MSG). Jesus saw how hard the Pharisees pursued God through the law, but they missed that Jesus came to fulfill the law so they wouldn't have to. They missed that they were also outsiders who were sick and in need of a doctor. They were so focused on trying to please God all on their own that they missed God's offer of love and forgiveness extended to all people.

Jesus didn't care that Levi wasn't the Pharisees' type of guy; he called Levi to follow him anyway. No matter who we are, what we do, or where we're from, Jesus invites all of us to experience God's love, forgiveness, and hope, which brings new life and freedom.

PRAYER PROMPT

Today's story showed how Jesus invites everyone to know God's love. Let's thank God for that love and ask for God's forgiveness for the times when we've judged others as being unworthy of love and forgiveness. Let's ask God to show us the people in our lives—maybe even the unlikely ones—who deserve to know God's love and mercy. May we find ways to show that love and mercy to them.

ACTIVITY #1: DINNER PARTY

Who doesn't love to have a little party? Think about a neighbor, church family, or friend you've never invited to your home and plan a get-together with them. Sharing a meal with people is a great way to get to know people and show God's hospitality and love to them.

ACTIVITY #2: SELF-EXAMINATION

The Pharisees couldn't see that they needed Jesus just like Levi needed Jesus. But we all fall short of the glory of God, don't we? What are some ways you know you need the love and forgiveness of God? Take an honest look at yourself in the presence of God, who shows mercy and forgiveness, not harsh judgment for our failures. You can always confess those short-comings and thank God that the Holy Spirit is with you always, helping you be the best version of yourself.

Tax Collectors and "Sinners"

The Pharisees often gave Jesus a hard time for hanging out with "sinners." They expected Jesus, a fellow teacher, to spend time with people who were dedicated to trying to be holy, like them. Instead, Jesus said that he came to seek and to save the lost. But why would a job like tax collecting lump you in with "sinners"? A Jewish tax collector would not have been well-liked by fellow Jews. During biblical times, the Jews and the Romans did not get along at all; in fact, they hated one another. The Romans were foreign rulers and occupiers of Jewish land, and Levi's job was to collect money from his Jewish neighbors and turn it over to the Romans. It's no surprise that the Pharisees looked down their noses at Levi, but it *is* surprising that Jesus embraced him as one of his disciples!

Pigs, Demons, Gentiles, and Jesus

SETTING UP THE STORY

In the last two stories, we've met some of the people Jesus chose as his disciples to follow him and learn from him. Some were friends and relatives and fishermen, and others were people with bad reputations in the community. So far, they've all been part of the same community and of the same religion (Jesus and his disciples were all Jewish). In today's story, Jesus traveled to an area where mostly Gentiles (or non-Jewish people) lived, and he encountered a man possessed by demons. Otherworldly things happen!

READ: MARK 5:1–20 (NLT)

So they arrived at the other side of the lake, in the region of the Gerasenes. When Jesus climbed out of the boat, a man possessed by an evil spirit came out from the tombs to meet him. This man lived in the burial caves and could no longer be restrained, even with a chain. Whenever he was put into chains and shackles—as he often was—he snapped the chains from his wrists and smashed the shackles. No one was strong enough to subdue him. Day and night he wandered among the burial caves and in the hills, howling and cutting himself with sharp stones.

When Jesus was still some distance away, the man saw him, ran to meet him, and bowed low before him. With a shriek, he screamed, "Why are you interfering with me, Jesus, Son of the Most High God? In the name of God, I beg you, don't torture me!" For Jesus had already said to the spirit, "Come out of the man, you evil spirit."

Then Jesus demanded, "What is your name?"

And he replied, "My name is Legion, because there are many of us inside this man." Then the evil spirits begged him again and again not to send them to some distant place.

There happened to be a large herd of pigs feeding on the hillside nearby. "Send us into those pigs," the spirits begged. "Let us enter them."

So Jesus gave them permission. The evil spirits came out of the man and entered the pigs, and the entire herd of about two thousand pigs plunged down the steep hillside into the lake and drowned in the water.

The herdsmen fled to the nearby town and the surrounding countryside, spreading the news as they ran. People rushed out to see what had happened. A crowd soon gathered around Jesus, and they saw the man who had been possessed by the legion of demons. He was sitting there fully clothed and perfectly sane, and they were all afraid. Then those who had seen what happened told the others about the demon-possessed man and the pigs. And the crowd began pleading with Jesus to go away and leave them alone.

As Jesus was getting into the boat, the man who had been demon possessed begged to go with him. But Jesus said, "No, go home to your family, and tell them everything the Lord has done for you and how merciful he has been." So the man started off to visit the Ten Towns of that region and began to proclaim the great things Jesus had done for him; and everyone was amazed at what he told them.

TALK ABOUT IT

- What was the demon-possessed man like before he encountered Jesus? How did he change after Jesus drove the demons out of him?
- Imagine being one of the herdsmen who watched the pigs stampede off the cliff. How do you think they felt about what happened? What was their reaction?
- How does the crowd react when they find out about the healing of the demon-possessed man and the pigs?
- Why didn't Jesus let the man who had been demon possessed go with him as a disciple?

- What happened as a result of the man staying in the area instead of going with Jesus?
- Is there anything that confuses you about this story? If so, it's okay! Let's talk about it.
- Do you have any questions about Mark 5:1–20?

CLOSING THOUGHT

If you are wide-eyed about today's story, you aren't alone—today's story is wild! A man possessed by a demon, the demon that called himself "Legion," a herd of pigs diving off a cliff . . . there's a lot in today's story that seems otherworldly. And it is!

Jesus demonstrated his power over the spiritual world and the natural world in today's story. When Jesus told the demons to leave the man, they obeyed. God has power over everything in creation, and in this moment, as the Son of God, Jesus showed a community of people what God was like.

This story takes place in an area where mostly Gentiles lived. Whenever possible, Jews and Gentiles did not spend time together, but Jesus often broke down the barriers between people in order to show God's great love for all. The demon-possessed man was a dangerous outcast, known in the community for his violence. When Jesus encountered him, he did not shun him or turn him away; he saw his needs and rescued him. As a result, one man's life was changed forever and a whole community learned about the wonders of God.

PRAYER PROMPT

The Holy Spirit is with us always, to comfort and to change our hearts. Let's thank God for that life-changing work, and ask God to continue to renew a right spirit within us. Let's also pray that God would allow us to see the outcasts in our society through his eyes.

ACTIVITY #1: BEFORE AND AFTER

The demon-possessed man was very different after he met Jesus. Use the time-lapse function on your phone to record yourself cleaning a messy room or completing a chore, like doing the dishes or folding laundry. Once you're done, watch the fast-speed before-and-after transformation!

ACTIVITY #2: CARING FOR THE OUTCAST

Talk with your family about people in your community who might be considered outsiders. Find out what your church or other organizations in your community are doing to help meet the needs of people, and decide as a family how you can serve. You could serve at a soup kitchen, donate to a food pantry, or give new or gently used items to a homeless shelter. Be creative and be bold!

The Region of the Gerasenes and the Ten Towns

Mostly Gentiles lived in the area Jesus traveled to in today's story. The region of the Gerasenes was on the southeast side of the Sea of Galilee. The people in the story were probably not Jews, since Jews were not permitted by their religious laws to raise or eat pork. Many of the gospel stories involve Jesus talking to Jews, but there are also stories like this one that show Jesus talking to and changing the lives of Gentiles. At the end of the story, the man healed by Jesus goes out into the "Ten Towns" to tell people about what happened to him. This group of ten cities was known as the Decapolis.[1] As a result of the demon-possessed man's life-changing encounter, a whole region learned about God's power and love.

Healing People Left and Right

SETTING UP THE STORY

The trend of Jesus healing and teaching unlikely disciples continues in today's story. As we keep reading stories from the Gospels to learn how God wants us to love others, it's important to pay attention to whom Jesus interacts with, where they are from, and what they learn from him. God does more miraculous deeds in today's story. Let's dive in!

READ: MARK 5:21–43 (NIV)

When Jesus had again crossed over by boat to the other side of the lake, a large crowd gathered around him while he was by the lake. Then one of the synagogue leaders, named Jairus, came, and when he saw Jesus, he fell at his feet. He pleaded earnestly with him, "My little daughter is dying. Please come and put your hands on her so that she will be healed and live." So Jesus went with him.

A large crowd followed and pressed around him. And a woman was there who had been subject to bleeding for twelve years. She had suffered a great deal under the care of many doctors and had spent all she had, yet instead of getting better she grew worse. When she heard about Jesus, she came up behind him in the crowd and touched his cloak, because she thought, "If I just touch his clothes, I will be healed." Immediately her bleeding stopped and she felt in her body that she was freed from her suffering.

At once Jesus realized that power had gone out from him. He turned around in the crowd and asked, "Who touched my clothes?"

"You see the people crowding against you," his disciples answered, "and yet you can ask, 'Who touched me?'"

But Jesus kept looking around to see who had done it. Then the woman, knowing what had happened to her, came and fell at his feet and, trembling with fear, told him the whole truth. He said to her, "Daughter, your faith has healed you. Go in peace and be freed from your suffering."

While Jesus was still speaking, some people came from the house of Jairus, the synagogue leader. "Your daughter is dead," they said. "Why bother the teacher anymore?"

Overhearing what they said, Jesus told him, "Don't be afraid; just believe."

He did not let anyone follow him except Peter, James and John the brother of James. When they came to the home of the synagogue leader, Jesus saw a commotion, with people crying and wailing loudly. He went in and said to them, "Why all this commotion and wailing? The child is not dead but asleep." But they laughed at him.

After he put them all out, he took the child's father and mother and the disciples who were with him, and went in where the child was. He took her by the hand and said to her, "*Talitha koum!*" (which means "Little girl, I say to you, get up!"). Immediately the girl stood up and began to walk around (she was twelve years old). At this they were completely astonished. He gave strict orders not to let anyone know about this, and told them to give her something to eat.

TALK ABOUT IT

- What healed the woman in the crowd?
- When people told Jairus that his daughter was dead, what did Jesus say to him?
- Why do you think Jesus didn't want anyone to talk about his healing the little girl?
- How would you react if someone who was really sick suddenly became well, or someone who had died came back to life?
- Is there anything that confuses you about this story? If so, it's okay! Let's talk about it.
- Do you have any questions about Mark 5:21–43?

CLOSING THOUGHT

Two kinds of people interact with Jesus in today's story. Jairus, the synagogue leader who approached Jesus about his dying daughter, would have been well-respected and powerful. And then there's a random, sick woman. Women were not highly regarded in biblical times.

Right in the middle of going to see Jairus's daughter, the sick woman grabbed Jesus's clothes, hoping to be healed. Jewish rules said that anyone who touched a bleeding woman was considered unclean. This woman had bled for twelve years! That's a long time to be considered untouchable.

According to Jewish law, after the woman touched Jesus, he should have washed his clothes and taken a bath to be clean again. Instead, Jesus sought her out and told her that her faith had healed her.

If that wasn't enough, Jesus went on to touch a dead girl . . . and bring her back to life! Again, Jesus defied Jewish purity rules in order to heal. God's love extends beyond the expected to reach the unexpected. God's love is for everyone!

PRAYER PROMPT

God's great power extends to us when we're suffering. If we are struggling, hurt, sad, or sick, we can ask God for comfort and healing. Let's thank God for his big grace and giant love that always makes time for us.

ACTIVITY #1: LITTLE GIRL, GET UP!

Take turns acting out what happened in the room with Jairus's daughter. How do you think her parents reacted? What about the disciples who were there watching?

ACTIVITY #2: COMFORT THE SUFFERING

Jesus doesn't run away from those who are sick or dying; he goes to their side to help them out. It can feel weird and scary to be around someone who isn't well, but Jesus calls us to help those who need help. If there is someone in your life who is sick right now, think about a creative way you can comfort them. If you can't be with them, write a handmade card, pick out a special treat or gift for them, or give them a call to let them know you are thinking of them and praying for them. Your words and actions can be just the kind of healing they need right now.

Twelve Years of Suffering, Twelve Years Old

Numbers carry a lot of meaning in the Bible. In today's story, the woman healed had bled for twelve years, and the girl who was raised from the dead was twelve years old. What is the significance of the number twelve, and why are these two stories paired together?

The number twelve in Judaism symbolizes wholeness and the completion of God's purpose.[2] In both situations in today's story, Jesus broke Jewish laws: women who bled would have been considered unclean, and touching a dead person was considered unclean. Jesus broke those rules in order to heal and to show people that God's love and power cover over all people at all times. By mentioning the years the woman had suffered and how old the little girl was, the writer of this story made sure readers understood that Jesus was fulfilling God's purpose.

Eating and Drinking the Rules Away

SETTING UP THE STORY

We learned in the last devotional that Jesus went out of his way to help those who sought him out, even to the point of breaking long-established religious rules in order to save the hurting. The Pharisees didn't like this behavior very much, as we'll discover in today's story. Let's see how Jesus talked to the Pharisees about their concerns and what he had to say to his disciples afterward.

READ: MARK 7:1–23 (NLT)

One day some Pharisees and teachers of religious law arrived from Jerusalem to see Jesus. They noticed that some of his disciples failed to follow the Jewish ritual of hand washing before eating. (The Jews, especially the Pharisees, do not eat until they have poured water over their cupped hands, as required by their ancient traditions. Similarly, they don't eat anything from the market until they immerse their hands in water. This is but one of many traditions they have clung to—such as their ceremonial washing of cups, pitchers, and kettles.)

So the Pharisees and teachers of religious law asked him, "Why don't your disciples follow our age-old tradition? They eat without first performing the hand-washing ceremony."

Jesus replied, "You hypocrites! Isaiah was right when he prophesied about you, for he wrote,

'These people honor me with their lips,
but their hearts are far from me.
Their worship is a farce,
for they teach man-made ideas as commands from God.'

For you ignore God's law and substitute your own tradition."

Then he said, "You skillfully sidestep God's law in order to hold on to your own tradition. For instance, Moses gave you this law from God: 'Honor your father and mother,' and 'Anyone who speaks disrespectfully of father or mother must be put to death.' But you say it is all right for people to say to their parents, 'Sorry, I can't help you. For I have vowed to give to God what I would have given to you.' In this way, you let them disregard their needy parents. And so you cancel the word of God in order to hand down your own tradition. And this is only one example among many others."

Then Jesus called to the crowd to come and hear. "All of you listen," he said, "and try to understand. It's not what goes into your body that defiles you; you are defiled by what comes from your heart."

Then Jesus went into a house to get away from the crowd, and his disciples asked him what he meant by the parable he had just used. "Don't you understand either?" he asked. "Can't you see that the food you put into your body cannot defile you? Food doesn't go into your heart, but only passes through the stomach and then goes into the sewer." (By saying this, he declared that every kind of food is acceptable in God's eyes.)

And then he added, "It is what comes from inside that defiles you. For from within, out of a person's heart, come evil thoughts, sexual immorality, theft, murder, adultery, greed, wickedness, deceit, lustful desires, envy, slander, pride, and foolishness. All these vile things come from within; they are what defile you."

TALK ABOUT IT

- What does Jesus have to say to the Pharisees when they complain about his disciples not following the rules?
- What do you think Jesus meant when he said, "It's not what goes into your body that defiles you; you are defiled by what comes from your heart"?

- Jesus isn't shy about confronting the Pharisees or correcting the disciples when it comes to these purification rituals. How do you think the Pharisees and the disciples felt after hearing Jesus say these things?
- Is there anything that confuses you about this story? If so, it's okay! Let's talk about it.
- Do you have any questions about Mark 7:1–23?

CLOSING THOUGHT

All the rules and cleaning rituals in Judaism served to set apart the Jews from the rest of the world. Some of those rules told the Jews what they should and should not eat. The swine in the story about the demon-possessed man were an example of one kind of food that was off-limits to Jews. (That means no bacon, all you meat eaters!) Jesus pointed out that the traditions and rules are easier to focus on than the most important laws: to love God and to love others.

The rules and rituals that were intended to bring us closer to God and to others sometimes cause more separation. Jesus came to refocus our hearts and minds on loving God and loving others. By doing so, he opened access to God from just the Jews to everyone, whether or not they ate the right things or obeyed the right rules. Because God loves each of us dearly, he cares the most about our hearts and how we treat others.

PRAYER PROMPT

Let's pray this together: God, forgive us for the times we've emphasized obeying a set of rules over taking care of each other. Help us to love one another, learn your ways for living a good life, and acknowledge when we're in the wrong so that we can make things right with others. Thank you for your constant and never-changing love for us, that corrects us when we make mistakes and welcomes us back into your embrace.

ACTIVITY #1: NEW HOUSE RULES

You probably have some common rules in your home, and these are important to follow. Sometimes we get so focused on following the rules that we forget the reason why they are there in the first place. On a piece of paper, make two columns, one titled "Love God" and the other titled "Love Others." Discuss your house rules and where each of your rules fits on your paper. Hang your list somewhere in your house to remind you and your family about the heart behind your house rules.

ACTIVITY #2: ADVENTURE BITE

The Pharisees were real sticklers about what they would eat and drink and when, but Jesus didn't make such a big deal about food, saying that purity isn't about what you put into your body but what's inside your heart. Try something new this week: eat food that you wouldn't normally eat—pick out a recipe or ingredient your family has never tried before and prepare a meal together as a family.

God's Law

In Matthew 22:37–40 (NLT), Jesus told the Pharisees and religious teachers that there are two commandments that are the most important: "'You must love the Lord your God with all your heart, all your soul, and all your mind.' This is the first and greatest commandment. A second is equally important: 'Love your neighbor as yourself.' The entire law and all the demands of the prophets are based on these two commandments." Jesus used these two commandments to show his followers what God expects. "Honor your father and mother" is one of the Ten Commandments in the Old Testament and is referenced in today's reading. Like Jesus said, each of the Ten Commandments can be summarized by these two: loving God and loving our neighbors as ourselves.

Table Scraps and Hungry Disciples

SETTING UP THE STORY

On the heels of instructing the Pharisees and disciples about clean and unclean foods, Jesus encountered a woman who was not Jewish, begging for help. Have you noticed this trend in the Gospels? The people Jesus came from—the Jews and religious folks—were often bewildered and confused by him, but all the unlikely disciples were hungry for his healing and his love. While many of the Jews mocked him, some of the Gentiles flocked to him! Today's story continues that trend.

READ: MARK 7:24–37 (MSG)

From there Jesus set out for the vicinity of Tyre. He entered a house there where he didn't think he would be found, but he couldn't escape notice. He was barely inside when a woman who had a disturbed daughter heard where he was. She came and knelt at his feet, begging for help. The woman was Greek, Syro-Phoenician by birth. She asked him to cure her daughter.

He said, "Stand in line and take your turn. The children get fed first. If there's any left over, the dogs get it."

She said, "Of course, Master. But don't dogs under the table get scraps dropped by the children?"

Jesus was impressed. "You're right! On your way! Your daughter is no longer disturbed. The demonic affliction is gone." She went home and found her daughter relaxed on the bed, the torment gone for good.

Then he left the region of Tyre, went through Sidon back to Galilee Lake and over to the district of the Ten Towns. Some people brought a man who could neither hear nor speak and asked Jesus to lay a healing hand on him. He took the man off by himself, put his fingers in the man's ears and some spit on the man's tongue. Then Jesus looked up in prayer, groaned mightily, and commanded, "*Ephphatha!*—Open up!" And it happened. The man's hearing was clear and his speech plain—just like that.

Jesus urged them to keep it quiet, but they talked it up all the more, beside themselves with excitement. "He's done it all and done it well. He gives hearing to the deaf, speech to the speechless."

TALK ABOUT IT

- Do you ever just want to get away from others for a little while? How do you think Jesus felt when the Greek woman found him?
- Jesus has some seemingly harsh words at first for the Greek woman. Why do you think he said these things to her?
- How does Jesus handle people who are constantly interrupting his day?
- What do you think the deaf and mute man's life was like before he met Jesus, and how do you think he felt after he was given his hearing and speech?
- Why do you think Jesus kept telling people to keep quiet about the miracles he performed?
- Is there anything that confuses you about this story? If so, it's okay! Let's talk about it. Do you have any questions about Mark 7:24–37?

CLOSING THOUGHT

There goes Jesus again, spending time with people who don't fit the mold! Any time we read these stories, we have to remember that Jesus was Jewish, and the Jews believed that God had set them apart as his people. The Jews did whatever they could to remain separate from the Gentile (non-Jewish) people. On top of that, the culture prohibited men and women from talking to one another in public.[3]

Instead of following these customs, Jesus went to where non-Jewish people lived and spent time with people who weren't like him. After healing the Greek woman's daughter, Jesus went back to the region of the Ten Towns. That's the area where the demon-possessed man lived. Word had spread since Jesus drove out the demon called Legion, and now the people of the area were the ones who brought someone to Jesus to be healed.

Jesus didn't avoid people who weren't like him. He crossed borders. He defied race and gender rules. He broke social boundaries. He did it all to show God's love for everyone, and to show God's people how they should love others.

PRAYER PROMPT

The Greek woman boldly asked Jesus for help. The people of the Ten Towns boldly brought the deaf and mute man to Jesus. God receives every one of our requests, no matter how big or impossible they might seem. Pray boldly for God's help, thank him for the ways he has helped your family, and ask him to reveal ways you can be a helper to others.

ACTIVITY #1: BE A HELPER

As carriers of the Holy Spirit we are Jesus's representatives on earth. Look and listen for the Holy Spirit's nudge to help someone this week.

ACTIVITY #2: EXPLORE A PARK

Jesus traveled around to different areas and met new people as a result. Find a playground or park in your area that you've never been to and see if you can make new friends with someone you wouldn't have asked to play before.

The Children and the Dogs

Many stories of Jesus discussing the law with the Jews are followed by stories of Jesus connecting with and healing the Gentiles. Jesus came first to the Jew, and then to the Gentile. The Jews didn't always receive him, but many of the Gentiles did. The disciples would have heard Jesus's harsh words and recognized them as their own deeply held prejudices about Gentiles and women. The conversation between the Greek woman and Jesus revealed to the disciples (and all who would read the story later) that Jesus's gift of salvation is for *all*, even people whom the world might not think are worthy.[4]

The Power of Believing Jesus

SETTING UP THE STORY

After Jesus called together his disciples, he sent the twelve of them out into the world to begin doing miraculous works. They could drive out demons, just like Jesus. They could heal the sick, just like Jesus. They could help the hurting, just like Jesus. So while Jesus went up a mountain to retreat with three of his closest disciples (and witness miraculous events—check out the first part of Mark 9 to read that story), the other disciples stayed back, continuing the work of Jesus. Let's find out what happened next.

READ: MARK 9:14–29 (NIV)

When they came to the other disciples, they saw a large crowd around them and the teachers of the law arguing with them. As soon as all the people saw Jesus, they were overwhelmed with wonder and ran to greet him.

"What are you arguing with them about?" he asked.

A man in the crowd answered, "Teacher, I brought you my son, who is possessed by a spirit that has robbed him of speech. Whenever it seizes him, it throws him to the ground. He foams at the mouth, gnashes his teeth and becomes rigid. I asked your disciples to drive out the spirit, but they could not."

"You unbelieving generation," Jesus replied, "how long shall I stay with you? How long shall I put up with you? Bring the boy to me."

So they brought him. When the spirit saw Jesus, it immediately threw the boy into a convulsion. He fell to the ground and rolled around, foaming at the mouth.

Jesus asked the boy's father, "How long has he been like this?"

"From childhood," he answered. "It has often thrown him into fire or water to kill him. But if you can do anything, take pity on us and help us."

"'If you can'?" said Jesus. "Everything is possible for one who believes."

Immediately the boy's father exclaimed, "I do believe; help me overcome my unbelief!"

When Jesus saw that a crowd was running to the scene, he rebuked the impure spirit. "You deaf and mute spirit," he said, "I command you, come out of him and never enter him again."

The spirit shrieked, convulsed him violently and came out. The boy looked so much like a corpse that many said, "He's dead." But Jesus took him by the hand and lifted him to his feet, and he stood up.

After Jesus had gone indoors, his disciples asked him privately, "Why couldn't we drive it out?"

He replied, "This kind can come out only by prayer."

TALK ABOUT IT

- What did the father in the story think about Jesus and his ability to heal his son?
- How did the father's approach to Jesus differ from some of the other stories we've read about healing so far?
- What do you think the father meant when he said, "I do believe; help me overcome my unbelief"?
- Why do you think Jesus was frustrated with the crowd and the disciples?
- How do you think the disciples felt when Jesus was able to heal the boy but they weren't?
- Is there anything that confuses you about this story? If so, it's okay! Let's talk about it.
- Do you have any questions about Mark 9:14–29?

CLOSING THOUGHT

When Jesus and the other three disciples returned to their community from being on the top of a mountain, they came back to an argument between the disciples, the Pharisees, and others from the Jewish community.

After all that had happened already, Jesus was frustrated that they still didn't understand what he was all about.

Jesus told the disciples in private that this type of demon can only come out through prayer. The Jewish community had a very hard time understanding the things Jesus was doing, and that unbelief got in the way of their ability to love others. When we don't believe something is possible, it becomes impossible.

When we keep turning to God as the source of our strength, our courage, and our wisdom, God will keep lifting us up and giving us the faith to love, help, and restore others in ways we never dreamed could be possible. God gives us what we need, if we just believe.

PRAYER PROMPT

Let's thank God for meeting us wherever we are, even in the middle of unbelief and doubt. Ask God to help you with any questions you have about who Jesus is and what the Lord requires of you. When we encounter situations that make us doubt whether we can make a difference, ask God to give you the belief and the strength to overcome your fears.

ACTIVITY #1: BELIEVE BIG

What's something that's hard to believe could be a reality for you or your family? Dream big. Believe big. Jesus told the father, "Everything is possible for one who believes." Decorate a poster with the words, "Believe Big" in the middle. If you're feeling extra crafty, make a collage of pictures that illustrate what you think God's love looks like in the world.

ACTIVITY #2: HELP MY UNBELIEF

In today's story, nearly everyone thought the boy was beyond helping, even the disciples. The father saw how valuable his son was, and so did Jesus. If you encounter someone who believes negative things about themselves, try to help them overcome their unbelief to see themselves the way Jesus sees them. Look for opportunities to encourage your friends and family.

Believe/Unbelief

The father's statement, "I do believe; help me overcome my unbelief," seems like a contradiction—how can you both believe *and* want help with your unbelief? The word *believe* is the Greek verb *pisteuō*,[5] and the word *unbelief* is the Greek noun *apistia*.[6] As a verb, believing is an action. It isn't something you *have*, it's something you *do*. But unbelief is a noun. It's something you will *have*—doubts and questions about God—at times in your life. Those unbeliefs can be overcome through the active work of believing, or trusting, that God is who he says he is.

Let the Little Children Come to Jesus!

SETTING UP THE STORY

The disciples had a lot to learn about God from Jesus compared with what they always thought, and Jesus was never shy about correcting them. In so many ways, Jesus turned the world upside down when he came. We've seen how Jesus welcomed people who were looked down on by others. In today's story, the disciples learn another world-changing lesson.

READ: MARK 9:33–50; 10:13–16 (NLT)

After they arrived at Capernaum and settled in a house, Jesus asked his disciples, "What were you discussing out on the road?" But they didn't answer, because they had been arguing about which of them was the greatest. He sat down, called the twelve disciples over to him, and said, "Whoever wants to be first must take last place and be the servant of everyone else."

Then he put a little child among them. Taking the child in his arms, he said to them, "Anyone who welcomes a little child like this on my behalf welcomes me, and anyone who welcomes me welcomes not only me but also my Father who sent me."

John said to Jesus, "Teacher, we saw someone using your name to cast out demons, but we told him to stop because he wasn't in our group."

"Don't stop him!" Jesus said. "No one who performs a miracle in my name will soon be able to speak evil of me. Anyone who is not against us is for us. If anyone gives you even a cup of water because you belong to the Messiah, I tell you the truth, that person will surely be rewarded.

"But if you cause one of these little ones who trusts in me to fall into sin, it would be better for you to be thrown into the sea with a large millstone hung around your neck. If your hand causes you to sin, cut it off. It's better to enter eternal life with only one hand than to go into the unquenchable fires of hell with two hands. If your foot causes you to sin, cut it off. It's better to enter eternal life with only one foot than to be thrown into hell with two feet. And if your eye causes you to sin, gouge it out. It's better to enter the Kingdom of God with only one eye than to have two eyes and be thrown into hell, 'where the maggots never die and the fire never goes out.'

"For everyone will be tested with fire. Salt is good for seasoning. But if it loses its flavor, how do you make it salty again? You must have the qualities of salt among yourselves and live in peace with each other." . . .

One day some parents brought their children to Jesus so he could touch and bless them. But the disciples scolded the parents for bothering him.

When Jesus saw what was happening, he was angry with his disciples. He said to them, "Let the children come to me. Don't stop them! For the Kingdom of God belongs to those who are like these children. I tell you the truth, anyone who doesn't receive the Kingdom of God like a child will never enter it." Then he took the children in his arms and placed his hands on their heads and blessed them.

TALK ABOUT IT

- What do you think Jesus meant when he said, "Whoever wants to be first must take last place and be the servant of everyone else"?
- What are some ways you can be "the servant of everyone else"?
- Jesus said hard things about sinning in the middle of today's story. Do you think Jesus *really* meant you should cut off your hand or your foot to keep from sinning? If not, what do you think he meant?
- How did Jesus feel about children?
- How does the way Jesus talked about children make you feel?
- Is there anything that confuses you about this story? If so, it's okay! Let's talk about it.
- Do you have any questions about Mark 9:33–50; 10:13–16?

CLOSING THOUGHT

For as long as anyone can remember, people have decided who belongs and who should be left out. When the disciples argued about who should have the most power, Jesus told them the person with the least power, a servant, would be first. When the disciples tried to stop someone who wasn't in their group from performing miracles in Jesus's name, Jesus told them that anyone who wasn't against them was for them. And when the disciples tried to keep children away from Jesus so they wouldn't be a distraction from more important things, Jesus got angry.

Jesus was done with the "God Club," where you had to have the right parents, look a certain way, be a certain age, and follow certain rules to be a member. Jesus is available to everyone. God values every life and doesn't want anyone left out from experiencing his love.

When you feel left out, Jesus says, "Come to me." When you feel neglected, Jesus says, "You are precious." When you feel unworthy of love, Jesus says, "I love you no matter what." Jesus expected the disciples to treat people the exact same way.

PRAYER PROMPT

Let's thank God for his big love for everyone and ask him to help us invite others into that love. If there is anyone you feel like you have a hard time loving the way God loves them, pray for the Holy Spirit to help you see them through his eyes as another child of God in need of his love. Pray for help finding ways to show God's love to that person.

ACTIVITY #1: HOW I LOVE YOU

At the end of the story today, Jesus put his hands on the children's heads and blessed them. Parents, place your hands on your child, look into their eyes, and tell them about your love and God's love: "I love you. You are worthy of love and attention. You are precious to me, and you are precious to God. I will always love you, no matter what, and God will always love you, no matter what."

ACTIVITY #2: CATCH

Jesus didn't want his love kept from anyone. Share the love with your family by playing a game of catch.

Cut Your Arm Off?!

Some of the teachings of Jesus can seem strange and, well, pretty extreme. If your right hand causes you to sin, you should cut it off?! Really? No, not really. The culture in biblical times relied heavily on hyperbole, or exaggeration, to make a point. We do the same thing when we say things like, "I'd rather die than eat broccoli!" or "I'm so hungry I could eat a horse!" Exaggerated speech tells the listener just how serious you are, more so than "I don't like broccoli" or "I'm hungry." That's how we can know just how serious Jesus was about not blocking people from God's love.

Just Do It; I Believe in You

SETTING UP THE STORY

Children, women, tax collectors, sinners, people from other cultures and backgrounds, sick people, demon-possessed people . . . Jesus kept surprising his disciples with the kinds of people he was more than willing to help, to heal, and to love. In today's story, Jesus surprised them again with not only whom he chose to heal but why he chose to heal them.

READ: LUKE 7:1–10 (MSG)

When he finished speaking to the people, he entered Capernaum. A Roman captain there had a servant who was on his deathbed. He prized him highly and didn't want to lose him. When he heard Jesus was back, he sent leaders from the Jewish community asking him to come and heal his servant. They came to Jesus and urged him to do it, saying, "He deserves this. He loves our people. He even built our meeting place."

Jesus went with them. When he was still quite far from the house, the captain sent friends to tell him, "Master, you don't have to go to all this trouble. I'm not that good a person, you know. I'd be embarrassed for you to come to my house, even embarrassed to come to you in person. Just give the order and my servant will get well. I'm a man under orders; I also give orders. I tell one soldier, 'Go,' and he goes; another, 'Come,' and he comes; my slave, 'Do this,' and he does it."

Taken aback, Jesus addressed the accompanying crowd: "I've yet to come across this kind of simple trust anywhere in Israel, the very people who are supposed to know about God and how he works." When the messengers got back home, they found the servant up and well.

TALK ABOUT IT

- Why did the Jewish leaders want Jesus to heal the Roman captain's servant?
- How do you imagine a Roman captain might be? What might he be like?
- How does the Roman captain describe himself in contrast to Jesus?
- What caused the Roman captain's servant to be healed?
- Is there anything that confuses you about this story? If so, it's okay! Let's talk about it.
- Do you have any questions about Luke 7:1–10?

CLOSING THOUGHT

The Romans in Capernaum were not friendly with the Jewish community. In fact, the Jews and the Romans were each other's enemies. A Roman captain held a lot of power and influence in the community. Based on this story, the Jewish leaders must have established a good relationship with the Roman captain. They felt it was to their advantage for Jesus to help out the Roman captain.

The Jews believed Jesus should heal the Roman captain's servant because the captain was someone who had done good things for the Jewish community. But Jesus chose to heal the man's servant because of the Roman captain's faith.

Jesus doesn't base his love off of whether or not someone "deserves it" or whether someone has earned it. He doesn't help people so that they'll do him a favor later. He just keeps on loving people, the powerful and the powerless, rich and poor alike. Jesus looks beyond the surface of a person into their heart.

PRAYER PROMPT

Let's pray together: Lord, thank you for not showing favoritism based on how much money a person makes, how much power they have, or what they look like. Help us to love people the way you love people. Forgive us for the times we've been generous or helpful only because it benefited us. Help us believe in your power the way the Roman captain believed.

ACTIVITY #1: SIMON SAYS

The Roman captain understood the power Jesus had to just say the word, and whatever Jesus said would be done. Play a game of Simon Says and see who can last the longest obeying the leader's instructions.

ACTIVITY #2: HELP THE HELPLESS

The servant in the story today was so sick he couldn't go to Jesus himself, so the Roman captain sought out Jesus for him. Is there someone in your life who is struggling right now that could use some help? Figure out a way you can help them, whether by visiting or calling, making a meal or a treat, writing a card, or giving a gift.

The Roman Servant

Today's story referred to the Roman captain's servant, but many other Bible translations call him a slave. Slavery was very common in ancient civilizations. People were enslaved for several reasons, most commonly as prisoners of war or as punishment for a crime or a debt they owed. Slaves were viewed as the lowest rank of society, yet Jesus doesn't look down on him. He healed him anyway. Paul, one of Jesus's apostles, wrote, "There is no longer Jew or Gentile, slave or free, male and female. For you are all one in Christ Jesus" (Galatians 3:28 NLT). Even though the world around Jesus used slaves (and sadly continued to enslave people for centuries), Jesus came to give freedom and unity to all. Sometimes humanity is slow to catch up with the revolutionary work of God.

Look Who's Coming to Dinner at Simon the Pharisee's House

SETTING UP THE STORY

We keep reading stories where Jesus encounters two types of people—the Jews, who were God's people of promise, and others who were left out of that promise. The way Jesus interacts with both groups sends the same message over and over: God's love is so much bigger than what everyone thought. Even though this is good news, the Jews struggled to accept Jesus's message because it didn't fit their understanding of God. Let's see how Jesus handled a situation with another guest at Simon the Pharisee's house.

READ: LUKE 7:36–50 (NIV)

When one of the Pharisees invited Jesus to have dinner with him, he went to the Pharisee's house and reclined at the table. A woman in that town who lived a sinful life learned that Jesus was eating at the Pharisee's house, so she came there with an alabaster jar of perfume. As she stood behind him at his feet weeping, she began to wet his feet with her tears. Then she wiped them with her hair, kissed them and poured perfume on them.

When the Pharisee who had invited him saw this, he said to himself, "If this man were a prophet, he would know who is touching him and what kind of woman she is—that she is a sinner."

Jesus answered him, "Simon, I have something to tell you."

"Tell me, teacher," he said.

"Two people owed money to a certain moneylender. One owed him five hundred denarii, and the other fifty. Neither of them had the money to pay him back, so he forgave the debts of both. Now which of them will love him more?"

Simon replied, "I suppose the one who had the bigger debt forgiven."

"You have judged correctly," Jesus said.

Then he turned toward the woman and said to Simon, "Do you see this woman? I came into your house. You did not give me any water for my feet, but she wet my feet with her tears and wiped them with her hair. You did not give me a kiss, but this woman, from the time I entered, has not stopped kissing my feet. You did not put oil on my head, but she has poured perfume on my feet. Therefore, I tell you, her many sins have been forgiven—as her great love has shown. But whoever has been forgiven little loves little."

Then Jesus said to her, "Your sins are forgiven."

The other guests began to say among themselves, "Who is this who even forgives sins?"

Jesus said to the woman, "Your faith has saved you; go in peace."

TALK ABOUT IT

- What are some common things you do to welcome a guest into your home?
- Why was Simon upset about the woman and Jesus?
- How does Jesus compare Simon the Pharisee and the woman?
- What does Jesus say about forgiveness and love?
- Is there anything that confuses you about this story? If so, it's okay! Let's talk about it.
- Do you have any questions about Luke 7:36–50?

CLOSING THOUGHT

The woman in today's story came to bless the man who set her free with the message of God's love for sinners. No one had heard that message before. In everyone else's view, including the Pharisees, it was only those who were righteous (or good) that God cared about, not sinners.

Simon, a keeper of the law, was shocked by this woman's behavior. The Pharisees had worked long and hard to be good enough for God's love, and they had strong opinions about how much people should have to work to earn that love. On top of that, they were astonished that Jesus accepted her offering as if he had the power to forgive sins. Only God can do that!

Simon expected Jesus to be just as offended by the woman. Instead, Jesus told Simon a parable about God's forgiveness of *all debts, big and small*. In big ways and little ways, both Simon and the woman had fallen short, but God's forgiveness is for all. Jesus opened the door for both the woman and Simon to accept that forgiveness.[7]

PRAYER PROMPT

Think back over the last week. Has there been a time when you have judged someone else for doing wrong? Let's admit (or confess) to each other and to God what we've judged, ask for forgiveness, and thank God for forgiving all sins, big and small. Praise God for his great love that covers over every sin!

ACTIVITY #1: THE WELCOMED GUEST

Simon the Pharisee, Jesus, and the nameless woman would have made for strange company, but sometimes the most powerful conversations come about when different people eat together. Plan a time to invite over two other families who don't know each other yet. You could be a bridge to better friendships!

ACTIVITY #2: ALABASTER JAR

An alabaster jar held precious perfumes and important objects during biblical times. Think about the things you are grateful for or the people you hold dear in your life. Find a vase or empty jar. On slips of paper, write down what you're grateful for and put them into your jar. When you are feeling sad or down, pour out those blessings and look through them to remember again how much God loves you.

Common Courtesies for House Guests

There are common greetings every culture practices to make people feel welcome, and when those practices don't happen, we can be made to feel unwelcome. The same was true during Jesus's time. While we might shake hands or give a hug to greet a guest, Jewish custom required a kiss of greeting, usually on the face. Then guests were offered olive oil and water to clean their hands and feet.[8] When Simon didn't offer either of these common courtesies, everyone there realized this was an intentional insult. Jesus didn't become offended but used the insult to show Simon the power of God's forgiveness for all sins.[9]

Changing a Woman's Place

SETTING UP THE STORY

We continue to learn about the ways Jesus connected with unlikely disciples in today's story about Mary and Martha. Any time women are mentioned in the Bible, it is important to remember that the culture at the time did not see women as equals to men. Rabbis (Jewish teachers) wouldn't be caught dead talking to a woman in public, not even to the female members of their own families![10] Every time Jesus interacted with women, we should take notice. There's a reason for this story.

READ: LUKE 10:38–42 (NLT)

As Jesus and the disciples continued on their way to Jerusalem, they came to a certain village where a woman named Martha welcomed him into her home. Her sister, Mary, sat at the Lord's feet, listening to what he taught. But Martha was distracted by the big dinner she was preparing. She came to Jesus and said, "Lord, doesn't it seem unfair to you that my sister just sits here while I do all the work? Tell her to come and help me."

But the Lord said to her, "My dear Martha, you are worried and upset over all these details! There is only one thing worth being concerned about. Mary has discovered it, and it will not be taken away from her."

TALK ABOUT IT

- What was Mary doing at the feet of Jesus?
- Why was Martha upset?
- How do you feel when other people seem to be having a good time but you have a chore to do?
- What is the "one thing" that Jesus says is worth being concerned about?

- Is there anything that confuses you about this story? If so, it's okay! Let's talk about it.
- Do you have any questions about Luke 10:38–42?

CLOSING THOUGHT

It was unheard of in Jesus's time for women to sit at the feet of a religious teacher like Jesus, and Martha knew it.[11] It could be said in ancient Middle Eastern culture, "A woman's place is in the kitchen." When Mary sat down with the rest of the (male) disciples to learn from Jesus, she broke all of the societal norms. Martha, and probably the other disciples, would have expected Jesus to agree with her—Mary needed to accept her role as a woman and get back into the kitchen!

But, shocker! Jesus didn't do that. Once again, Jesus broke with tradition and social codes of conduct to praise and encourage Mary's desire to learn from him.

We can make all kinds of assumptions about who should be allowed to do something and who should be left out, but Jesus ignored all of that and opened the door for everyone to know God, regardless of race or gender.

PRAYER PROMPT

Let's thank God for the invitation to know him better. No matter how old or young we are, or what gender we are, or what race we are, or how rich or poor we are, God's love is for everyone, and God invites us to extend it to everyone. Let's pray that God would show us where we've thought too small about his great love.

ACTIVITY #1: PLAN A SABBATH

Jesus challenged Martha to accept that it was more than okay for Mary to sit at Jesus's feet and learn from him. This week, take a break from the busyness as a family and plan a Sabbath, or day of rest. Take a walk together, explore a park, play a board game, or choose your own restful activity that will help you connect with each other and with God.

ACTIVITY #2: AT JESUS'S FEET

You've all been learning lots of things about Jesus. Take turns teaching your favorite Jesus stories to your other family members. When it's your turn to be the teacher, stand up and tell the story in your own words. When it's your turn to be the listener, sit at the teacher's feet. Which do you like to do the most, be the teacher or be the listener?

Martha's House

It's tempting to think about Martha as the villain in the story, stuck in the old ways of "women's work" while Mary studied at Jesus's feet. But at the beginning of today's story, we learn that this was Martha's house. During biblical times, women rarely owned property. Martha owned this house. Jesus frequently returned to her home throughout his life. He found warmth and hospitality at Martha's home. While Mary became one of Jesus's disciples, Martha had the gift of caring for his needs, and Jesus sought the comfort of Martha's home regularly throughout his ministry. Both women were highly valued and deeply loved by Jesus.

That's a Whole Lot of Love

SETTING UP THE STORY
In today's story, we're back visiting with Martha, Mary, and their brother, Lazarus. Not too long before this visit, Jesus had raised Lazarus from the dead (check out John 11:1–44 for that amazing miracle). Things were downright tense between Jesus and the religious leaders by this point, and the disciples were all worried about being near Jerusalem for fear that Jesus might be arrested or killed. But there was more that Jesus wanted to teach his disciples.

READ: JOHN 12:1–11 (MSG)
Six days before Passover, Jesus entered Bethany where Lazarus, so recently raised from the dead, was living. Lazarus and his sisters invited Jesus to dinner at their home. Martha served. Lazarus was one of those sitting at the table with them. Mary came in with a jar of very expensive aromatic oils, anointed and massaged Jesus' feet, and then wiped them with her hair. The fragrance of the oils filled the house.

Judas Iscariot, one of his disciples, even then getting ready to betray him, said, "Why wasn't this oil sold and the money given to the poor? It would have easily brought three hundred silver pieces." He said this not because he cared two cents about the poor but because he was a thief. He was in charge of their common funds, but also embezzled them.

Jesus said, "Let her alone. She's anticipating and honoring the day of my burial. You always have the poor with you. You don't always have me."

Word got out among the Jews that he was back in town. The people came to take a look, not only at Jesus but also at Lazarus, who had been raised from the dead. So the high priests plotted to kill Lazarus because so many of the Jews were going over and believing in Jesus on account of him.

TALK ABOUT IT

- What is your impression of Mary in this story?
- Why did Judas get upset about the oil?
- What is the best gift someone has ever given you? What does that gift mean to you?
- How do you think Lazarus felt about being brought back to life?
- Why do you think the high priests were angry that so many people were believing in Jesus because of Lazarus?
- Is there anything that confuses you about this story? If so, it's okay! Let's talk about it.
- Do you have any questions about John 12:1–11?

CLOSING THOUGHT

There's a whole lot of love going on in Martha's house! Lazarus doesn't say much in these stories, but I bet you can imagine how much he loved Jesus for bringing him back to life, and how grateful Martha and Mary must have been. From the earlier story of Martha and Mary, you already know that Mary was valued as one of Jesus's disciples. She obviously loved him deeply.

And then there's Judas, the scheming apostle about to betray Jesus.

Like the nameless woman in the story of Simon the Pharisee, Mary's display made the whole house uncomfortable. She let down her hair, she poured out super-expensive perfume on Jesus's feet, and then she rubbed his feet. This was simply unheard of.

And like Simon the Pharisee, Judas was appalled and irritated by the over-the-top expression of adoration. But Jesus didn't scold Mary. Instead, Jesus sided with Mary's extravagant, bold, intimate display of love. In the face of the reserved and calculating eye of a scheming disciple, love stands with the wild and shameless.

PRAYER PROMPT

Let's praise God a little differently today! In the Old Testament, King David "danced with great abandon before God" (2 Samuel 6:14 MSG), and in today's story, Mary poured out her most expensive oil on Jesus's feet to show her love and adoration. Parents and children, choose some music and sing and dance to God, praising him for his great love and affection!

ACTIVITY #1: THE AROMAS OF MEMORY

The oil used by Mary was a very powerful oil called "nard." The overpowering aroma of the oil would have filled the whole room. Scents are a powerful trigger for memories. The next time the disciples smelled nard, they probably remembered that scene with Mary and Jesus. What are some aromas that bring back memories for you?

ACTIVITY #2: EXTRAVAGANT GIFTS

The perfume that Mary poured on Jesus's feet would have been worth the equivalent of one year's wages. How much money is that for your family? Brainstorm with your family what kind of gifts you would buy for each other with that kind of money. It's fun to dream!

The Poor Are Always with You

If we didn't know from the gospel writer that Judas was scheming to steal from the disciples and betray Jesus, we'd probably feel the same way he did about the expensive oil. Couldn't that oil have been used for the poor? When Jesus said, "You always have the poor with you," he may have been referencing an Old Testament passage, "Give freely and spontaneously. Don't have a stingy heart. The way you handle matters like this triggers GOD, your God's, blessing in everything you do, all your work and ventures. There are always going to be poor and needy people among you. So I command you: Always be generous, open purse and hands, give to your neighbors in trouble, your poor and hurting neighbors" (Deuteronomy 15:10–11 MSG). Jesus knew Judas's heart. He wanted that money for himself. God commands us to always be generous.

Salvation Is for Everyone, Even the Oppressors

SETTING UP THE STORY

Many of the unlikely disciples so far seem to fit a certain character description: they are undeserving, poor, not the religious elite, oppressed, and outcasts. The religious leaders and the crowd could rally around the good feelings they had when Jesus overcame their prejudices and healed the oppressed. But what about when Jesus saves the oppressor?

READ: LUKE 19:1–10 (NIV)

Jesus entered Jericho and was passing through. A man was there by the name of Zacchaeus; he was a chief tax collector and was wealthy. He wanted to see who Jesus was, but because he was short he could not see over the crowd. So he ran ahead and climbed a sycamore-fig tree to see him, since Jesus was coming that way.

When Jesus reached the spot, he looked up and said to him, "Zacchaeus, come down immediately. I must stay at your house today." So he came down at once and welcomed him gladly.

All the people saw this and began to mutter, "He has gone to be the guest of a sinner."

But Zacchaeus stood up and said to the Lord, "Look, Lord! Here and now I give half of my possessions to the poor, and if I have cheated anybody out of anything, I will pay back four times the amount."

Jesus said to him, "Today salvation has come to this house, because this man, too, is a son of Abraham. For the Son of Man came to seek and to save the lost."

TALK ABOUT IT

- What do you think about a grown man running ahead of a crowd and climbing a tree?
- Why did Jesus decide to stay with Zacchaeus?
- Why do you think the crowd was upset with Jesus for staying at Zacchaeus's house?
- What do you think the crowd expected Jesus to say to Zacchaeus?
- What motivated Zacchaeus to suddenly be generous?
- Is there anything that confuses you about this story? If so, it's okay! Let's talk about it.
- Do you have any questions about Luke 19:1–10?

CLOSING THOUGHT

No one in town liked Zacchaeus much. As Jericho's wealthy chief tax collector, Zacchaeus was rich and powerful and a collaborator with Rome. By definition, Zacchaeus was one who oppressed the Jewish people.

And yet, here's Zacchaeus, running ahead of the crowd to climb a tree to catch a glimpse of this prophet, teacher, and Messiah. Even though the whole community wrote off Zacchaeus as a scoundrel, Jesus loved him and invited him into a relationship. The crowds were appalled, again, by this scandalous grace that kept violating their expectations of who deserved God's love.

Zacchaeus accepted Jesus's love, and out of that love, Zacchaeus was motivated to try to repay the wrongs he had done. In response, Jesus declared that salvation had already come to his house—no matter what Zacchaeus did next, his acceptance of Jesus's costly grace was enough. Salvation was already there, in the flesh. Jesus came to seek and to save the lost, even the lost chief tax collectors and sinners like Zacchaeus.

PRAYER PROMPT

Let's thank God that his love is for all of us. From that outpouring of love comes a changed life; ask God to continue working on you to become the most complete version of yourself. Pray for those who seem unforgivable for their behavior in your life, that they might find God and be saved the way Jesus saved Zacchaeus in today's story.

ACTIVITY #1: TYPES OF TREES

The Bible is very specific about the type of tree Zacchaeus climbed. A sycamore-fig tree grew on the outskirts of town. It had branches easy to climb and broad leaves that could conceal someone.[12] God cares about specifics like that. Take a walk around your neighborhood and see how many different trees you can identify. Collect a leaf from each and study the level of detail that goes into each and every living thing.

ACTIVITY #2: PRAYER LIST

Zacchaeus and many other unlikely disciples in the Bible had their lives interrupted and changed forever because of Jesus. Make a list of people (perhaps no more than five) you hope will accept God's love and grace. Commit to praying for those people regularly. Prayer is powerful! Who knows what might happen?

Just Passing Through

Jesus was said to be just "passing through" Jericho at the beginning of the story today. Middle Eastern culture would have expected Jesus to stay the night, so the crowds with Jesus were likely disappointed that Jesus wasn't hanging out with them in Jericho that evening. Jesus added insult to injury when he decided to stay after all, in the house of a known "sinner"![13] On top of everything else, it was the eve of Passover. Because Zacchaeus worked with Romans to collect taxes, he was considered unclean according to Jewish purification rules. If Jesus stayed with Zacchaeus, he would have been considered unclean too. By the time Zacchaeus was declaring his commitment to be generous and give back to the community, the crowd would have been furious with Jesus. Everything he did went against their customs and their rules, but Jesus kept on loving anyway, seeking and saving the lost.

Who Was with Jesus at His Crucifixion?

SETTING UP THE STORY

We have seen how Jesus chose a band of unlikely disciples to receive his grace and tell his story, and that trend continued all the way up to his crucifixion. Let's find out who accompanied Jesus during his time of suffering on the cross, and how he interacted with them even when he was in great pain. This is the darkest part of Jesus's journey, but we have the advantage of knowing the rest of the story, the amazing miracle of his resurrection.

READ: JOHN 19:25–42 (NLT)

Standing near the cross were Jesus's mother, and his mother's sister, Mary (the wife of Clopas), and Mary Magdalene. When Jesus saw his mother standing there beside the disciple he loved, he said to her, "Dear woman, here is your son." And he said to this disciple, "Here is your mother." And from then on this disciple took her into his home.

Jesus knew that his mission was now finished, and to fulfill Scripture he said, "I am thirsty." A jar of sour wine was sitting there, so they soaked a sponge in it, put it on a hyssop branch, and held it up to his lips. When Jesus had tasted it, he said, "It is finished!" Then he bowed his head and gave up his spirit.

It was the day of preparation, and the Jewish leaders didn't want the bodies hanging there the next day, which was the Sabbath (and a very special Sabbath, because it was Passover week). So they asked Pilate to hasten their deaths by ordering that their legs be broken. Then their bodies could be taken down. So the soldiers came and broke the legs of the two men crucified with Jesus. But when they came to Jesus, they saw that he was already dead, so they didn't break his legs. One of the soldiers, however, pierced his side with a spear, and immediately blood and water flowed out. (This report is from an eyewitness giving an accurate account. He speaks the truth so that you also may continue to believe.) These things happened in fulfillment of the Scriptures that say, "Not one of his bones will be broken," and "They will look on the one they pierced."

Afterward Joseph of Arimathea, who had been a secret disciple of Jesus (because he feared the Jewish leaders), asked Pilate for permission to take down Jesus' body. When Pilate gave permission, Joseph came and took the body away. With him came Nicodemus, the man who had come to Jesus at night. He brought about seventy-five pounds of perfumed ointment made from myrrh and aloes. Following Jewish burial custom, they wrapped Jesus' body with the spices in long sheets of linen cloth. The place of crucifixion was near a garden, where there was a new tomb, never used before. And so, because it was the day of preparation for the Jewish Passover and since the tomb was close at hand, they laid Jesus there.

TALK ABOUT IT

- Who were the people at the cross when Jesus was being crucified?
- Who do you think was the "disciple [Jesus] loved"?
- Do you know who *wasn't* at the cross when Jesus was crucified?
- Who prepared Jesus's body for burial?
- Why do you think Joseph was afraid of the Jewish leaders?
- Is there anything that confuses you about this story? If so, it's okay! Let's talk about it.
- Do you have any questions about John 19:25–42?

CLOSING THOUGHT

After Jesus was arrested in the garden of Gethsemane, all of the other disciples fled. The only disciples who remained by Jesus's side at the time of his death were a few women and John (he's the "disciple [Jesus] loved").

Nicodemus and Joseph came to collect Jesus's body. They were both members of the Jewish council. Earlier in Jesus's ministry, Nicodemus came to talk to Jesus under the cover of night (John 3). Joseph was a secret follower of Jesus because he feared the other Jews. Even though Joseph and Nicodemus kept their interest in Jesus a secret, they still returned to the cross to care for his body.

What side of history would we have been on as Jesus's disciples? Would we have been like the women? Would we have been like those who abandoned Jesus? Would we have been secret followers?

On the Sunday morning that followed this dark day, Jesus rose from the dead and everything changed. No matter what mistakes or fears came before, they were washed away by his love and forgiveness.

PRAYER PROMPT

Let's thank God that he is patient with each of us as we journey through this world. Even when we are afraid or turn the other way, God is always seeking after us, looking out for us, and waiting for us to return to his love and grace. Let's pray for the courage to stand up for what is right, even if it isn't popular.

ACTIVITY #1: COMFORT THE GRIEVING

Matthew 5:4 says that those who mourn will be comforted. If you know someone who has lost a loved one, come up with a way to comfort them—send flowers, prepare a meal, or draw a picture. You choose how you want to tell them that they are loved by God. If you don't know someone, ask your pastor or an adult if there is someone in your community who could use some encouragement. We can even comfort strangers in their grief.

ACTIVITY #2: CARRYING EACH OTHER'S BURDENS

Even though Jesus conquered death, the disciples didn't know what was going to come next after his crucifixion. Take turns sharing with each other about a time you've been very sad. Maybe you even thought something was hopeless. How did it turn out? Who helped you through? Afterward, pray again together to thank God for the gift of loved ones who care for us when we're sad and hurting.

Dear Woman, Here Is Your Son

In Jewish tradition, as Mary's firstborn son, Jesus was responsible for the care of his mother after her husband was gone. Knowing that he was going to die, Jesus passed on this responsibility to one of his closest disciples. Mary had other children, but we know from other stories in the Gospels that they were not as supportive of Jesus's ministry. John accepted the ministry of Jesus and his leadership, and so he assumed the role of providing for Mary after Jesus died.

Section 2

THE DISCIPLES AND JESUS

The People with Jesus and the Parables He Shared

SETTING UP THE STORY

We all interact with different groups of people daily. We walk by people who are strangers to us. There are classmates and neighbors who know our names but probably don't know much more about us than that. Then there are our friends and family members who know us best. The disciples were Jesus's band of brothers and sisters who knew him best. They walked with Jesus and learned a lot from him. We can learn a lot about God's love for others through Jesus's love for his disciples, beginning with how Jesus explained things to them.

READ: LUKE 8:1–15 (NIV)

After this, Jesus traveled about from one town and village to another, proclaiming the good news of the kingdom of God. The Twelve were with him, and also some women who had been cured of evil spirits and diseases: Mary (called Magdalene) from whom seven demons had come out; Joanna the wife of Chuza, the manager of Herod's household; Susanna; and many others. These women were helping to support them out of their own means.

While a large crowd was gathering and people were coming to Jesus from town after town, he told this parable: "A farmer went out to sow his seed. As he was scattering the seed, some fell along the path; it was trampled on, and the birds ate it up. Some fell on rocky ground, and when it came up, the plants withered because they had no moisture. Other seed fell among thorns, which grew up with it and choked the plants. Still other seed fell on good soil. It came up and yielded a crop, a hundred times more than was sown."

When he said this, he called out, "Whoever has ears to hear, let them hear."

His disciples asked him what this parable meant. He said, "The knowledge of the secrets of the kingdom of God has been given to you, but to others I speak in parables, so that,

"'though seeing, they may not see;

though hearing, they may not understand.'

"This is the meaning of the parable: The seed is the word of God. Those along the path are the ones who hear, and then the devil comes and takes away the word from their hearts, so that they may not believe and be saved. Those on the rocky ground are the ones who receive the word with joy when they hear it, but they have no root. They believe for a while, but in the time of testing they fall away. The seed that fell among thorns stands for those who hear, but as they go on their way they are choked by life's worries, riches and pleasures, and they do not mature. But the seed on good soil stands for those with a noble and good heart, who hear the word, retain it, and by persevering produce a crop."

TALK ABOUT IT

- Why were the women following Jesus?
- What do you think Jesus meant when he said, "Whoever has ears to hear, let them hear"?
- Who is the farmer in the parable of the sower?
- What are the seeds Jesus talked about?
- What are the four types of soil in Jesus's explanation of the parable?
- Is there anything that confuses you about this story? If so, it's okay! Let's talk about it.
- Do you have any questions about Luke 8:1–15?

CLOSING THOUGHT

It might not seem odd today, but in Jesus's time, it was highly unusual for men and women to travel to different cities together, for women to be paying for the trip, and on top of everything, for Luke to admit that this happened![1] Jesus's disciples included Jewish fishermen, tax collectors, a woman who had been demon possessed, a woman with political ties to Herod (the ruler who had John the Baptist killed for criticizing him), and many others. They had different backgrounds and jobs and genders. They all followed the same Lord.

Jesus taught that all kinds of people would hear the word of God, but not all would take it to heart. This is how it was for Jesus throughout his ministry and for centuries to come, even to today—some people hear the word of God and reject it outright. Some believe in the power of love until something tough happens, and then they turn away. Some embrace God's love but are lured away by power, pleasure, and wealth. And then there are those who hear the word and keep growing in love, no matter what may come.

PRAYER PROMPT

Let's pray that God's Spirit will soften our hearts and help us receive his word of love. Let's ask God to show us how to keep growing in that love through our day-to-day interactions with friends, neighbors, and strangers. Let's also pray for our church community to believe and act upon the message of love.

ACTIVITY #1: PLANT SOME SEEDS

With your family, pick out seed packets to plant some herbs for an indoor herb garden. Some good herbs to choose include basil, oregano, cilantro, rosemary, chives, mint, and thyme. You'll need some potting soil, a couple of pots, and a south-facing window or grow light.

ACTIVITY #2: A VERSE TO GROW BY

Decorate a sign with the last verse in today's story, "But the seed on good soil stands for those with a noble and good heart, who hear the word, retain it, and by persevering produce a crop." Draw what this verse means to you.

Parables

Jesus used short, instructional stories called parables to teach his followers about God and God's kingdom. Parables rely on metaphors to invite us into the mind of God so we can see the world through his eyes. The parables draw on the everyday experiences of the people who were listening. Through those familiar pictures, the crowds could understand the big ideas Jesus shared about who God is. They also painted a picture of how different God's kingdom looks compared with the world.

Go Boldly into the World, Disciples!

SETTING UP THE STORY

In the last devotional, Jesus taught his disciples the parable of the sower. Jesus uses a lot of stories about planting, growing, and getting ready to pick the fruits and vegetables at harvest time. In today's story, Jesus mentions harvesting again as the starting place for sending out his disciples. Jesus tells the disciples what it is going to be like to follow him, where they should go, how they should behave, and what to expect when they share the name of Jesus. If we are Jesus's disciples today, his message is for us as well!

READ: MATTHEW 9:35–38; 10:1–28 (MSG)

Then Jesus made a circuit of all the towns and villages. He taught in their meeting places, reported kingdom news, and healed their diseased bodies, healed their bruised and hurt lives. When he looked out over the crowds, his heart broke. So confused and aimless they were, like sheep with no shepherd. "What a huge harvest!" he said to his disciples. "How few workers! On your knees and pray for harvest hands!" . . .

The prayer was no sooner prayed than it was answered. Jesus called twelve of his followers and sent them into the ripe fields. He gave them power to kick out the evil spirits and to tenderly care for the bruised and hurt lives. This is the list of the twelve he sent:

Simon (they called him Peter, or "Rock"),
Andrew, his brother,
James, Zebedee's son,
John, his brother,
Philip,
Bartholomew,

Thomas,

Matthew, the tax man,

James, son of Alphaeus,

Thaddaeus,

Simon, the Canaanite,

Judas Iscariot (who later turned on him).

Jesus sent his twelve harvest hands out with this charge:

"Don't begin by traveling to some far-off place to convert unbelievers. And don't try to be dramatic by tackling some public enemy. Go to the lost, confused people right here in the neighborhood. Tell them that the kingdom is here. Bring health to the sick. Raise the dead. Touch the untouchables. Kick out the demons. You have been treated generously, so live generously.

"Don't think you have to put on a fund-raising campaign before you start. You don't need a lot of equipment. *You* are the equipment, and all you need to keep that going is three meals a day. Travel light.

"When you enter a town or village, don't insist on staying in a luxury inn. Get a modest place with some modest people, and be content there until you leave.

"When you knock on a door, be courteous in your greeting. If they welcome you, be gentle in your conversation. If they don't welcome you, quietly withdraw. Don't make a scene. Shrug your shoulders and be on your way. You can be sure that on Judgment Day they'll be mighty sorry—but it's no concern of yours now.

"Stay alert. This is hazardous work I'm assigning you. You're going to be like sheep running through a wolf pack, so don't call attention to yourselves. Be as shrewd as a snake, inoffensive as a dove.

"Don't be naive. Some people will question your motives, others will smear your reputation—just because you believe in me. Don't be upset when they haul you before the civil authorities. Without knowing it, they've done you—and me—a favor, given you a platform for preaching the kingdom news! And don't worry about what you'll say or how you'll say it. The right words will be there; the Spirit of your Father will supply the words.

"When people realize it is the living God you are presenting and not some idol that makes them feel good, they are going to turn on you, even people in your own family. There is a great irony here: proclaiming so much love, experiencing so much hate! But don't quit. Don't cave in. It is all well worth it in the end. It is not success you are after in such times but survival. Be survivors! Before you've run out of options, the Son of Man will have arrived.

"A student doesn't get a better desk than her teacher. A laborer doesn't make more money than his boss. Be content—pleased, even—when you, my students, my harvest hands, get the same treatment I get. If they call me, the Master, 'Dungface,' what can the workers expect?

"Don't be intimidated. Eventually everything is going to be out in the open, and everyone will know how things really are. So don't hesitate to go public now.

"Don't be bluffed into silence by the threats of bullies. There's nothing they can do to your soul, your core being. Save your fear for God, who holds your entire life—body and soul—in his hands."

TALK ABOUT IT

- How does Jesus tell the disciples to go about their mission?
- What were some of the things Jesus told the disciples to expect when they started talking about him to others?
- Have you ever had someone turn on you because of your love of Jesus? Share a story if you have one.
- How does Jesus's message make you feel about talking about your faith with others?
- If there's all these consequences for telling people about Jesus, why should we do it?
- Is there anything that confuses you about this story? If so, it's okay! Let's talk about it.
- Do you have any questions about Matthew 9:35–38; 10:1–28?

CLOSING THOUGHT

The message Jesus shared with his disciples sure is a mix of excitement and gloom, isn't it? You're going to be able to heal people and cast out demons, but also, people will hate you for it. There's so much power in the message of love, power to heal broken hearts and save broken lives. But Jesus also warned them: some people won't want to hear that message. Jesus didn't just say it *might* happen; he promised the disciples it *will* happen.

Some people will hate you because of the love you have for Jesus.

This shouldn't make us shy about loving people, though. As we go out into the world as his disciples, we need to be bold and unafraid, yet humble and kind. We shouldn't be showy about our message. We don't need a lot of preparation or extra money or education to share God's love with people. We just have to be willing to go and willing to face rejection, knowing that the Holy Spirit is going ahead of us, preparing hearts to receive the message of love and acceptance in Christ.

PRAYER PROMPT

Let's ask God to give us the courage and joy to be his disciples today and every day. If we're afraid of looking silly or not having the right words, let's pray for boldness and confidence that the Holy Spirit will show us what to say and do in every situation. Let's thank God that he is honest with us about what to expect from people so that we can be prepared to face those consequences, trusting that God is good and always with us, no matter what we face.

ACTIVITY #1: SHEEP, WOLVES, SNAKES, DOVES

Jesus told his disciples they should be like sheep among wolves, to be as shrewd as a snake and as innocent as a dove. Act out each animal and talk about why Jesus used these animals as examples in today's story.

ACTIVITY #2: GO PUBLIC!

What is one way you and your family members can "go public" with the message of Jesus this week? Ask God to nudge you during conversations at school and at work this week, and pray for the courage to listen up! Maybe God will show you someone who could use a word of encouragement, prayer, hope, or comfort.

The Compassion of Jesus

"When he looked out over the crowds, his heart broke." Wherever Jesus saw hurting, broken, and confused people, he had compassion for them. There was only so much he could do on his own, so Jesus recruited the disciples into action. The Son of God needed help spreading the message of love and healing people throughout the world. God calls us into that same care for the world today. Throughout Scripture, God's love shows up in kindness and compassion and calls his people to action.

Even More Hands
for the Harvest

SETTING UP THE STORY

After sending out his closest disciples, Jesus got another group ready to spread the message of hope and healing to area towns. Like he did with the first group, Jesus prepared them for what they should expect, but he also warned the disciples about what the towns should expect if they rejected the message about God.

READ: LUKE 10:1–20 (NLT)

The Lord now chose seventy-two other disciples and sent them ahead in pairs to all the towns and places he planned to visit. These were his instructions to them: "The harvest is great, but the workers are few. So pray to the Lord who is in charge of the harvest; ask him to send more workers into his fields. Now go, and remember that I am sending you out as lambs among wolves. Don't take any money with you, nor a traveler's bag, nor an extra pair of sandals. And don't stop to greet anyone on the road.

"Whenever you enter someone's home, first say, 'May God's peace be on this house.' If those who live there are peaceful, the blessing will stand; if they are not, the blessing will return to you. Don't move around from home to home. Stay in one place, eating and drinking what they provide. Don't hesitate to accept hospitality, because those who work deserve their pay.

"If you enter a town and it welcomes you, eat whatever is set before you. Heal the sick, and tell them, 'The Kingdom of God is near you now.' But if a town refuses to welcome you, go out into its streets and say, 'We wipe even the dust of your town from our feet to show that we have abandoned you to your fate. And know this—the Kingdom of God is near!' I assure you, even wicked Sodom will be better off than such a town on judgment day.

"What sorrow awaits you, Korazin and Bethsaida! For if the miracles I did in you had been done in wicked Tyre and Sidon, their people would have repented of their sins long ago, clothing themselves in burlap and throwing ashes on their heads to show their remorse. Yes, Tyre and Sidon will be better off on judgment day than you. And you people of Capernaum, will you be honored in heaven? No, you will go down to the place of the dead."

Then he said to the disciples, "Anyone who accepts your message is also accepting me. And anyone who rejects you is rejecting me. And anyone who rejects me is rejecting God, who sent me."

When the seventy-two disciples returned, they joyfully reported to him, "Lord, even the demons obey us when we use your name!"

"Yes," he told them, "I saw Satan fall from heaven like lightning! Look, I have given you authority over all the power of the enemy, and you can walk among snakes and scorpions and crush them. Nothing will injure you. But don't rejoice because evil spirits obey you; rejoice because your names are registered in heaven."

TALK ABOUT IT

- Why do you think Jesus encouraged the disciples to stay in one place when they found a home that welcomed them, instead of going from home to home?
- What does Jesus tell the disciples to do if people in a town reject them?
- Why do you think whole towns of people still rejected the message of Jesus, even after they saw him perform miracles?
- How does it make you feel to have "authority over all the power of the enemy"?
- Is there anything that confuses you about this story? If so, it's okay! Let's talk about it.
- Do you have any questions about Luke 10:1–20?

CLOSING THOUGHT

Building friendships with people takes time. Jesus encouraged the disciples to spend time with people who welcomed them. They should stay awhile, eat with them, and talk with them. If people didn't want the disciples around, Jesus told them to leave and let it be.

The message of Jesus Christ and the coming of the kingdom of God is powerful. God's love has the power to change many hearts, but it is not up to us to convince people that Jesus is Lord. It's up to us to show people the power of God's love. That's what it means to be a witness. When we show people God's love, we stand as an example of what God is like. That's what Jesus meant when he said that if people reject you, they also reject him.

Every person on earth has the choice to accept God's love or reject it. We are called to be Jesus's workers, the same way the disciples were called to share the message of God's love with people in today's story. If someone doesn't want to hear it, Jesus tells us we should let it go. Sometimes people aren't ready to hear the story of God's love.

PRAYER PROMPT

Lord, sometimes it feels like it is our job to convince people of your love. Thank you for showing us that it isn't all up to us. You are the One who saves people, and we get to be your messengers, showing how much you love us by loving others. Help us to remember that joy is contagious, love is patient, and hope does not disappoint us.

ACTIVITY #1: SPIRITUAL SUPERPOWERS

The disciples were super excited to be able to heal the sick and cast out demons. These spiritual superpowers are impressive! Draw or paint a picture of yourself as a spiritual superhero, or dress up as one.

ACTIVITY #2: A LITTLE SPRINKLE OF LOVE

Ask God to show you one person who could use a little sprinkle of God's love in their life this week. What can you say or do to encourage them? How can you show God's love to them?

The Cities of Unrepentance

Jesus had harsh words for Capernaum, Korazin, and Bethsaida. These were cities where Jesus and his disciples performed miracles and where some of the disciples lived. Capernaum was even the center of Jesus's public ministry for a while. If the people in these cities wouldn't accept Jesus's message and repent, who would? Jesus compared these three Jewish cities to places that were known for their wickedness in the Old Testament: Sodom, Tyre, and Sidon. All three of these cities were Gentile (or non-Jewish) towns. If *they* had seen the same miracles as the Jewish cities, Jesus says, they would have turned from their wicked ways. As a result, Jesus said that judgment would be even worse for these Jewish cities—which were filled with a bunch of people who were supposed to be following God but instead rejected him.

Teaching the Disciples How to Pray

SETTING UP THE STORY

Jesus spent a lot of time praying alone to God the Father. Wouldn't it be great to know how he talked to God, so that we can know how to talk to God? Thankfully, one of Jesus's disciples asked him about it! The Lord's Prayer is an often-memorized prayer repeated in church services around the world. We're going to read *The Message* version today, which might give you a little different understanding of the Lord's Prayer.

READ: LUKE 11:1–13 (MSG)

One day he was praying in a certain place. When he finished, one of his disciples said, "Master, teach us to pray just as John taught his disciples."

So he said, "When you pray, say,
> Father,
> Reveal who you are.
> Set the world right.
> Keep us alive with three square meals.
> Keep us forgiven with you and forgiving others.
> Keep us safe from ourselves and the Devil."

Then he said, "Imagine what would happen if you went to a friend in the middle of the night and said, 'Friend, lend me three loaves of bread. An old friend traveling through just showed up, and I don't have a thing on hand.'

"The friend answers from his bed, 'Don't bother me. The door's locked; my children are all down for the night; I can't get up to give you anything.'

"But let me tell you, even if he won't get up because he's a friend, if you stand your ground, knocking and waking all the neighbors, he'll finally get up and get you whatever you need.

"Here's what I'm saying:
> Ask and you'll get;
> Seek and you'll find;
> Knock and the door will open.

"Don't bargain with God. Be direct. Ask for what you need. This is not a cat-and-mouse, hide-and-seek game we're in. If your little boy asks for a serving of fish, do you scare him with a live snake on his plate? If your little girl asks for an egg, do you trick her with a spider? As bad as you are, you wouldn't think of such a thing—you're at least decent to your own children. And don't you think the Father who conceived you in love will give the Holy Spirit when you ask him?"

TALK ABOUT IT

- Why do you think we should pray to God?
- Can we ask God for things?
- What does Jesus tell us we should expect from God when we pray?
- Do you find it hard or easy to pray to God? Why?
- Is there anything that confuses you about this story? If so, it's okay! Let's talk about it.
- Do you have any questions about Luke 11:1–13?

CLOSING THOUGHT

Jesus taught his disciples the importance of praying to God. Built into the Lord's Prayer are all of the ways we can rely on him. We can count on God to show us who he is. We can ask him to bring peace and justice to the world. We can ask him to give us what we need to survive. We can seek his forgiveness when we've done wrong and ask for help forgiving others. And we can seek his protection, direction, and strength.

We can go to God with any worry or concern, any need, any desire. If we don't think God is listening, Jesus says to be persistent—keep praying, keep asking! If we keep talking to God, he will eventually answer. The answers might not always be what we hoped for—God isn't a genie in a bottle, after all—but he will answer.

Jesus told his disciples not to worry about fancy words or being shy; just come right out and tell God your thoughts, worries, joys, needs, and concerns. God listens and cares deeply about what is on your heart.

PRAYER PROMPT

Let's each take turns telling God what's on our hearts today.

ACTIVITY #1: PERSISTENT PRAYERS

Is there something you are worried about, something you need, or something you don't understand about God? Choose one thing you want to nag God about and pray about that one thing every day for a week. Share with your family what God revealed to you through your prayer time.

ACTIVITY #2: GOOD GIFT, BAD GIFT

Children, pretend you are the parent at the end of today's story and have your actual parent pretend to be a child. Pretend Child, ask your Pretend Parent for something good. Pretend Parent, go find a silly version of that gift for your Pretend Child. What silly gifts can you come up with, like the examples in the story?

Common Talk

When the Jewish people prayed to God, they used one specific language, Hebrew, their sacred language. Out in the streets of Judea, though, the common language of the people was Aramaic. When Jesus taught his disciples how to pray, he used the common language (Aramaic) instead of the sacred language (Hebrew).[2] Today, we sometimes get caught up on using the "right" words to pray to God or the "right" translation of the Bible to hear from God. But even the Son of God switched things up. As a result of Jesus's teaching, people of *all* languages can talk to God. People of *all* nations can hear from God. People of *all* walks of life can find God.

Living a Worry-Free Life

SETTING UP THE STORY

The stories Jesus told showed the disciples a picture of what God is like and how to live life God's way—the way of love. Some of the stories are hard for us, just like they were hard for the disciples and crowds who listened. Living God's way looks very different from the way most of the world lives, but if we trust God, then we know his way is good and perfect. Let's find out what Jesus has to say about money and worry.

READ: LUKE 12:13–34 (NIV)

Someone in the crowd said to him, "Teacher, tell my brother to divide the inheritance with me."

Jesus replied, "Man, who appointed me a judge or an arbiter between you?" Then he said to them, "Watch out! Be on your guard against all kinds of greed; life does not consist in an abundance of possessions."

And he told them this parable: "The ground of a certain rich man yielded an abundant harvest. He thought to himself, 'What shall I do? I have no place to store my crops.'

"Then he said, 'This is what I'll do. I will tear down my barns and build bigger ones, and there I will store my surplus grain. And I'll say to myself, "You have plenty of grain laid up for many years. Take life easy; eat, drink and be merry."'

"But God said to him, 'You fool! This very night your life will be demanded from you. Then who will get what you have prepared for yourself?'

"This is how it will be with whoever stores up things for themselves but is not rich toward God."

Then Jesus said to his disciples: "Therefore I tell you, do not worry about your life, what you will eat; or about your body, what you will wear. For life is more than food, and the body more than clothes. Consider the ravens: They do not sow or reap, they have no storeroom or barn; yet God feeds them. And how much more valuable you are than birds! Who of you by worrying can add a single hour to your life? Since you cannot do this very little thing, why do you worry about the rest?

"Consider how the wild flowers grow. They do not labor or spin. Yet I tell you, not even Solomon in all his splendor was dressed like one of these. If that is how God clothes the grass of the field, which is here today, and tomorrow is thrown into the fire, how much more will he clothe you—you of little faith! And do not set your heart on what you will eat or drink; do not worry about it. For the pagan world runs after all such things, and your Father knows that you need them. But seek his kingdom, and these things will be given to you as well.

"Do not be afraid, little flock, for your Father has been pleased to give you the kingdom. Sell your possessions and give to the poor. Provide purses for yourselves that will not wear out, a treasure in heaven that will never fail, where no thief comes near and no moth destroys. For where your treasure is, there your heart will be also."

TALK ABOUT IT

- What happened to the rich man in the story Jesus told the crowd?
- What do you think it means to be "rich toward God"?
- What things does Jesus tell his disciples they shouldn't worry about?
- What things do you worry about?
- What do you think is "a treasure in heaven"?
- Is there anything that confuses you about this story? If so, it's okay! Let's talk about it.
- Do you have any questions about Luke 12:13–34?

CLOSING THOUGHT

Living God's way looks different from the way most people live their lives. One of the biggest differences is how we are supposed to think about our money and possessions. Jesus called his disciples to hold on loosely to the things of this world. There is great freedom and peace for us when we don't have a tight grip on our money and things.

The rich man at the beginning of today's story tore down his buildings to try to store up riches for himself for the future, but God warned him that the future is unknown. Jesus encouraged his disciples to live worry-free, to remember that God is the one who takes care of our every need. How great it is that God knows our every need and cares for us!

The treasure Jesus encouraged his disciples to store up doesn't come in dollars and cents. Instead, its value is measured in kindness, joy, generosity, gratitude, mercy, and love. When we truly believe and trust that God is going to take care of all our needs, we are able to live out the call to love others generously, giving what we have with joy to those in need.

PRAYER PROMPT

We learned in the last devotional about the Lord's Prayer. In more traditional translations, part of the prayer says, "Give us this day our daily bread." When you pray together, ask God for what you need today and thank the Lord for how he always meets your daily needs.

ACTIVITY #1: GIVE GENEROUSLY

Choose a local charity to give to this week, trusting God to provide for and bless your family by living "rich toward God."

ACTIVITY #2: WILDFLOWERS AND RAVENS

Take a walk and look around at all the living things. Talk together about how God takes care of the plants and animals you see around you.

The Certain Rich Man

Jesus doesn't say that being wealthy is wrong. Instead, he pointed to the rich man's greed and selfishness. In the story, not once does the rich man consider God or others. It's all about him: "my land," "my barns," "my grain," "my crops," and "my future."[3] The rich man's focus is only on himself and his future, which it turns out, isn't going to last much longer. Jesus encouraged his disciples to open their hands, give generously, and live freely, so that no matter when their lives might be over, they would live investing in others instead of just themselves.

We Interrupt This Journey to Heal Someone

SETTING UP THE STORY

Jesus taught his followers how to ask God for things and what to expect from him. Jesus told his disciples to be persistent in their prayers, to ask for their heart's desire, and to expect that God would answer those prayers. Although the stories and situations changed, the root of his teaching to his disciples remained the same: love God and love others. Jesus never missed an opportunity to demonstrate what that love looked like, including in today's story.

READ: LUKE 18:35–43 (NLT)

As Jesus approached Jericho, a blind beggar was sitting beside the road. When he heard the noise of a crowd going past, he asked what was happening. They told him that Jesus the Nazarene was going by. So he began shouting, "Jesus, Son of David, have mercy on me!"

"Be quiet!" the people in front yelled at him.

But he only shouted louder, "Son of David, have mercy on me!"

When Jesus heard him, he stopped and ordered that the man be brought to him. As the man came near, Jesus asked him, "What do you want me to do for you?"

"Lord," he said, "I want to see!"

And Jesus said, "All right, receive your sight! Your faith has healed you." Instantly the man could see, and he followed Jesus, praising God. And all who saw it praised God, too.

TALK ABOUT IT

- How did the people with Jesus treat the blind beggar?
- Why do you think the crowd didn't want the blind beggar to talk to Jesus?
- Do you believe in miracles?
- Have you ever witnessed a miracle? Share a story if you have one.
- How do you think the blind man's life was changed after meeting Jesus?
- Is there anything that confuses you about this story? If so, it's okay! Let's talk about it.
- Do you have any questions about Luke 18:35–43?

CLOSING THOUGHT

At this point in Jesus's ministry, the people with Jesus had been listening to him and traveling with him for a long time. You would think they would realize by now that Jesus makes time for outcasts! Important people have places to be and things to do, and by every account, the crowd felt Jesus was an important person on his way to Jericho. The crowd didn't want that journey interrupted, so they tried to hush the blind beggar.

But Jesus lived for the interruptions. He always made time for people who cried out for him, especially the people the rest of the world looked down on and ignored. God makes space for interruptions. Wonders happen in the unscripted moments.

The journey wasn't going the way the crowd expected, but when they saw what Jesus was up to, they rejoiced! A blind man could now see! When we make room for Jesus to interrupt our day, we get to see miracles big and small happen in our own lives.

PRAYER PROMPT

Praise God for the holy interruptions! Lord, help us not to hurry through our days, blind to the opportunities you put in front of us to encourage or help someone in need. Forgive us for focusing only on the next thing to do instead of the next person you've put in our path that we could love. Thank you for showing us that your way pays more attention to the people than the set plan.

ACTIVITY #1: PARDON THE INTERRUPTION

As you go about your day, pay attention to the people around you. Ask God to open your eyes to interruption opportunities, moments when the Holy Spirit nudges you to say or do something for someone else. Report back to your family about the experience.

ACTIVITY #2: LEADING THE BLIND

Use a handkerchief or other piece of cloth to create a blindfold. Take turns guiding the blindfolded family member around the room by giving them verbal cues. After everyone has had a turn, consider searching online for organizations that help the blind and visually impaired and talking with your family about how you can support them.

Jesus, Son of David

When the blind beggar asked the crowd who was passing by, they identified Jesus as "the Nazarene." Jesus was from Nazareth, a town in Galilee. When introducing people, the Bible often tells where they are from to identify which person they are talking about. The beggar called Jesus by a different title: Son of David. According to the beginning of the book of Matthew, Jesus was a descendant of King David. The Old Testament promised the Messiah would be a descendant of David, so when the beggar identified Jesus as the Son of David, he proclaimed his belief that Jesus was the promised Messiah.[4]

What to Expect in Dark Days

SETTING UP THE STORY

Jesus knew the message of the gospel (good news) was going to rock the world. Because of this, he spent time preparing his disciples for what they should expect in the coming days. Let's learn what Jesus has to say about how we should respond when there's chaos and uncertainty in our world.

READ: MARK 13:1–13 (MSG)

As he walked away from the Temple, one of his disciples said, "Teacher, look at that stonework! Those buildings!"

Jesus said, "You're impressed by this grandiose architecture? There's not a stone in the whole works that is not going to end up in a heap of rubble."

Later, as he was sitting on Mount Olives in full view of the Temple, Peter, James, John, and Andrew got him off by himself and asked, "Tell us, when is this going to happen? What sign will we get that things are coming to a head?"

Jesus began, "Watch out for doomsday deceivers. Many leaders are going to show up with forged identities claiming, 'I'm the One.' They will deceive a lot of people. When you hear of wars and rumored wars, keep your head and don't panic. This is routine history, and no sign of the end. Nation will fight nation and ruler fight ruler, over and over. Earthquakes will occur in various places. There will be famines. But these things are nothing compared to what's coming.

"And watch out! They're going to drag you into court. And then it will go from bad to worse, dog-eat-dog, everyone at your throat because you carry my name. You're placed there as sentinels to truth. The Message has to be preached all across the world.

"When they bring you, betrayed, into court, don't worry about what you'll say. When the time comes, say what's on your heart—the Holy Spirit will make his witness in and through you.

"It's going to be brother killing brother, father killing child, children killing parents. There's no telling who will hate you because of me.

"Stay with it—that's what is required. Stay with it to the end. You won't be sorry; you'll be saved."

TALK ABOUT IT

- How does Jesus say we should respond to "doomsday deceivers"?
- Are there current events in the world that cause you to be afraid? What are they?
- What are some historical events that might have felt like the end of the world? Did the world end?
- How does Jesus's message about the world make you feel?
- What should we do when things in the world seem out of control?
- Is there anything that confuses you about this story? If so, it's okay! Let's talk about it.
- Do you have any questions about Mark 13:1–13?

CLOSING THOUGHT

Every generation has had a group of people who think the end of the world is near. It's true, a lot of awful things are happening, things that God hates, but there are also lots of beautiful things happening in the world, things that bring God glory and share God's light. When events seem to be spinning out of control, God reminds us that he has overcome the world. Light triumphs over darkness. Joy comes in the morning.

In today's story, Jesus warned the disciples about what they should expect as they share God's love. His warning is true for us too. We might meet people who don't really like to hear God's message of hope and love. It might make us uncomfortable. It might feel scary and confusing: why would anyone disagree with the message of love? In spite of that conflict,

Jesus encouraged his disciples and all who read his words to keep moving forward, to keep sharing God's message with the world. God's word is freedom and life. Take heart and be brave!

PRAYER PROMPT

Let's pray that God would give us courage and the ability to see his view of the world, to help us and encourage us when we feel frightened or anxious about what's happening around us. Thank God for his presence in all seasons.

ACTIVITY #1: HOUSE OF CARDS

Jesus talked about the temple falling down in today's story. Find a deck of cards or a box of blocks and work together to try to build a tall tower. Who can build the tallest tower before it falls down?

ACTIVITY #2: NEWS FAST

While it's important to know what's going on so that we know as Christians how to respond to the events of the world, sometimes we can get caught up in the anxiety and fear. Take a break from television, the news, and social media for a week. Choose other activities to do together as a family in its place, like playing a board game, taking a walk, or baking something.

The Temple's Destruction

Jesus told the disciples that the temple would fall within their lifetimes. In AD 70, about forty years after Jesus died and was resurrected, the temple, along with most of Jerusalem, was destroyed by the Romans in a siege.[5]

This was actually the Second Temple; the First Temple was built by Solomon. The temple was God's earthly house, the holy place Jews came to be nearest to God. It had stood in Jerusalem for over four hundred years and was destroyed by Nebuchadnezzar II in 587 BC.[6] About sixty years later, the Jews were allowed to return to Jerusalem following their exile. They immediately began rebuilding the Second Temple. The Second Temple stood in Jerusalem for nearly six hundred years before its destruction.

A new temple was never built, although Jews believe that someday a Third Temple will replace the Second. Christians believe that our bodies are God's temple for the Holy Spirit.

The Way to the Father

SETTING UP THE STORY

Throughout Jesus's ministry, we see him teach the disciples, heal the disciples, warn the disciples, serve the disciples, and scold the disciples. Jesus used all of his emotions with his disciples. We can expect to experience that same range of emotions with the ones we love the most. Today's story took place right before Jesus's arrest. In his final hours with the disciples, Jesus reassured them about how they could continue to find him, even after he was gone. He also explained to them how much he and God the Father are alike.

READ: JOHN 14:1–14 (NIV)

"Do not let your hearts be troubled. You believe in God; believe also in me. My Father's house has many rooms; if that were not so, would I have told you that I am going there to prepare a place for you? And if I go and prepare a place for you, I will come back and take you to be with me that you also may be where I am. You know the way to the place where I am going."

Thomas said to him, "Lord, we don't know where you are going, so how can we know the way?"

Jesus answered, "I am the way and the truth and the life. No one comes to the Father except through me. If you really know me, you will know my Father as well. From now on, you do know him and have seen him."

Philip said, "Lord, show us the Father and that will be enough for us."

Jesus answered: "Don't you know me, Philip, even after I have been among you such a long time? Anyone who has seen me has seen the Father. How can you say, 'Show us the Father'? Don't you believe that I am in the Father, and that the Father is in me? The words I say to you I do not speak on my own authority. Rather, it is the Father, living in me, who is doing his work. Believe me when I say that I am in the Father and the Father is in me; or at least believe on the evidence of the works themselves. Very truly I tell you, whoever believes in me will do the works I have been doing, and they will do even greater things than these, because I am going to the Father. And I will do whatever you ask in my name, so that the Father may be glorified in the Son. You may ask me for anything in my name, and I will do it."

TALK ABOUT IT

- How can we know God the Father?
- Do you think Philip and Thomas understood what Jesus was telling them?
- What do you think Jesus meant when he said, "I am the way and the truth and the life"?
- What evidence does Jesus give that he and the Father are the same?
- Is there anything that confuses you about this story? If so, it's okay! Let's talk about it.
- Do you have any questions about John 14:1–14?

CLOSING THOUGHT

People will sometimes say things like, "The apple doesn't fall far from the tree" or "Like father, like son." When it comes to Jesus and God, this is absolutely true! If we want to know who God the Father is, Jesus tells us to look at him, and we'll see the Father. As the Son of God walking around on earth, Jesus is such a gift to us because through him, we can know who God is and what God cares about.

We've read story after story of how Jesus makes room for people in his life, going out of his way to help others, heal others, teach others, feed others, and more. Through Jesus, we learn that the way to the God of love is to believe that Jesus is the Son of God and to live our lives the way he did: loving others abundantly.

PRAYER PROMPT

Let's thank God for Jesus. Thank him for all the ways Jesus shows us who God is, and name some of the characteristics of God that you see in Jesus.

ACTIVITY #1: A PLACE FOR YOU

Jesus is preparing a place for you in God's house. What do you think your room looks like? Share with your family members your dream room in God's house.

ACTIVITY #2: THE WAY

Jesus said that he is "the way and the truth and the life." Draw a path on a sheet of paper and write down things about Jesus that help you know that he is the Son of God. Write "Jesus is the way and the truth and the life" on your paper.

Thomas and Philip

Thomas and Philip, the two apostles who question Jesus in today's story, don't play major roles in the Gospels. They ask Jesus a couple of questions here and there, but they aren't counted among Jesus's inner circle. After Jesus's death and resurrection, Thomas is famous for doubting that Jesus could have come back to life but, upon seeing Jesus in the flesh, declared, "My Lord and my God!"

After Jesus was resurrected, Thomas and Philip are known historically for their work spreading the good news of Jesus. According to Christian tradition, Thomas traveled outside of the Roman Empire to teach about Jesus as far away as India with possible visits to China and Indonesia.[7] Philip was sent to preach in Greece, Phrygia, and Syria.[8] Although they both had quiet roles in the gospel stories, they lived active lives to share God's message of love with the world!

Come, Holy Spirit, Come!

SETTING UP THE STORY

Jesus's apostles were naturally distraught any time Jesus talked about leaving them. They had dedicated their lives and left their careers to follow Jesus the last three years. As Jesus approached the end of his ministry and neared his arrest, he felt it was necessary to prepare the disciples for what was about to happen. He loved his disciples and wanted them to be comforted. Jesus's message of hope for the disciples is a message of hope for us as well.

READ: JOHN 14:15–31 (NLT)

"If you love me, obey my commandments. And I will ask the Father, and he will give you another Advocate, who will never leave you. He is the Holy Spirit, who leads into all truth. The world cannot receive him, because it isn't looking for him and doesn't recognize him. But you know him, because he lives with you now and later will be in you. No, I will not abandon you as orphans—I will come to you. Soon the world will no longer see me, but you will see me. Since I live, you also will live. When I am raised to life again, you will know that I am in my Father, and you are in me, and I am in you. Those who accept my commandments and obey them are the ones who love me. And because they love me, my Father will love them. And I will love them and reveal myself to each of them."

Judas (not Judas Iscariot, but the other disciple with that name) said to him, "Lord, why are you going to reveal yourself only to us and not to the world at large?"

Jesus replied, "All who love me will do what I say. My Father will love them, and we will come and make our home with each of them. Anyone who doesn't love me will not obey me. And remember, my words are not my own. What I am telling you is from the Father who sent me.

I am telling you these things now while I am still with you. But when the Father sends the Advocate as my representative—that is, the Holy Spirit—he will teach you everything and will remind you of everything I have told you.

"I am leaving you with a gift—peace of mind and heart. And the peace I give is a gift the world cannot give. So don't be troubled or afraid. Remember what I told you: I am going away, but I will come back to you again. If you really loved me, you would be happy that I am going to the Father, who is greater than I am. I have told you these things before they happen so that when they do happen, you will believe.

"I don't have much more time to talk to you, because the ruler of this world approaches. He has no power over me, but I will do what the Father requires of me, so that the world will know that I love the Father. Come, let's be going."

TALK ABOUT IT
- What do you think an advocate is?
- How can we identify other people who follow Jesus?
- What does Jesus promise to give people who believe in him?
- How does it make you feel to know that the Holy Spirit is always with us?
- Is there anything that confuses you about this story? If so, it's okay! Let's talk about it.
- Do you have any questions about John 14:15–31?

CLOSING THOUGHT
The relationship between God the Father, Jesus the Son of God, and the Holy Spirit is one of the awesome mysteries of our faith. Jesus introduced the Holy Spirit in today's story and explained to the disciples how close the Holy Spirit will be to his followers—actually *in* them and with them always. That means that God truly is always with us, comforting us and guiding us. This is a big deal! When we trust God and believe in Jesus

Christ, we don't have to try to navigate our lives alone, because the Holy Spirit is in us, showing us the way of light and love.

Jesus told the disciples that the way you'll be able to tell who knows him is by how they obey his teachings and follow his commands. Jesus called his followers to love God and to love others; all of the other commandments are summarized in those two commands. As followers of Christ, we have the Holy Spirit with us to give us peace of mind and strength as we continue to follow those commands. How great it is that we have such a God, who promises to be with us always!

PRAYER PROMPT

Let's thank God for the presence of the Holy Spirit so that we can know God's love and feel that love close to us always. When we feel worried or afraid, we can put our trust in God, and the Holy Spirit will be right there giving us a peace that the world can't give. Let's also ask God to give us the courage and strength to keep obeying Jesus's words.

ACTIVITY #1: THREE IN ONE

God the Father, God the Son, and God the Holy Spirit are often called the Trinity, or three in one. Draw how you imagine their relationship.

ACTIVITY #2: A GIFT OF ADVOCACY

Is there a cause you feel strongly about individually or as a family? Find a way this week to advocate for, or publicly support, that cause for the good of God's kingdom. You can make a difference in the world; there's no cause too big or too small!

The Advocate

The Holy Spirit is called the "Advocate" by Jesus in today's story. An advocate is someone who is on your side and believes in you. They come to your defense. Their support is public. The word in Scripture that is translated here as "Advocate" is also translated "Comforter," "Encourager," or "Counselor."[9] The Holy Spirit is given to followers of Jesus to lead them into a deeper knowledge of who God is and to give them strength to handle anything the world throws at them. We can receive the Holy Spirit when we believe in our hearts that Jesus represents God's love on earth, and as Paul says in his letters to the early church, nothing can separate us from the love of God that is in Christ Jesus our Lord (Romans 8:38–39)!

How to Stay Connected to Jesus

SETTING UP THE STORY

Jesus promised that after he died and left them, the Holy Spirit would come and be with all of his followers. But relationships are two-way streets. While God's Holy Spirit lives in us, we have to do our part to stay connected, listen, and obey. In today's story, Jesus used a metaphor of a grapevine with branches to explain that relationship with God.

READ: JOHN 15:1–17 (MSG)

"I am the Real Vine and my Father is the Farmer. He cuts off every branch of me that doesn't bear grapes. And every branch that is grape-bearing he prunes back so it will bear even more. You are already pruned back by the message I have spoken.

"Live in me. Make your home in me just as I do in you. In the same way that a branch can't bear grapes by itself but only by being joined to the vine, you can't bear fruit unless you are joined with me.

"I am the Vine, you are the branches. When you're joined with me and I with you, the relation intimate and organic, the harvest is sure to be abundant. Separated, you can't produce a thing. Anyone who separates from me is deadwood, gathered up and thrown on the bonfire. But if you make yourselves at home with me and my words are at home in you, you can be sure that whatever you ask will be listened to and acted upon. This is how my Father shows who he is—when you produce grapes, when you mature as my disciples.

"I've loved you the way my Father has loved me. Make yourselves at home in my love. If you keep my commands, you'll remain intimately at home in my love. That's what I've done—kept my Father's commands and made myself at home in his love.

"I've told you these things for a purpose: that my joy might be your joy, and your joy wholly mature. This is my command: Love one another the way I loved you. This is the very best way to love. Put your life on the line for your friends. You are my friends when you do the things I command you. I'm no longer calling you servants because servants don't understand what their master is thinking and planning. No, I've named you friends because I've let you in on everything I've heard from the Father.

"You didn't choose me, remember; I chose you, and put you in the world to bear fruit, fruit that won't spoil. As fruit bearers, whatever you ask the Father in relation to me, he gives you.

"But remember the root command: Love one another."

TALK ABOUT IT
- What does it mean for a follower of Christ to "bear fruit"?
- How are we supposed to stay connected to Jesus?
- How would you describe your home? How does home feel?
- What is Jesus's command in today's story?
- Is there anything that confuses you about this story? If so, it's okay! Let's talk about it.
- Do you have any questions about John 15:1–17?

CLOSING THOUGHT
Today's story reinforces the message we've heard throughout the Gospels: stay connected to Jesus, live in God's love, and love others from within God's love. When we're living connected to God's love, we can expect to experience holy peace, joy, satisfaction, and rest. It's like being in the presence of your very best friend or safe at home with your family, only better—there are no secrets, only openness, full trust, and unconditional love. Out of that love grows the fruit, or actions, of love. As followers of Christ, we give the love we've received.

Anything we do that isn't rooted in God's love will be cut away by God as we grow and mature as followers of Christ. This is a lifelong process, not something that happens overnight. God will continue to shape and grow us throughout our lives, as long as we continue to seek out and live out his love. We are the ones who tend to move away from God, but he is patient with us and will continue to love us and be near us. To stay near to God, we are responsible for turning to him, listening to his words, and loving others the way he has loved us.

PRAYER PROMPT

Let's promise God that we will strive to live in his love. Thank God that he is ever near to us and always patient with us. It is wonderful to know God is always available and waiting for us to spend time with him. Let's ask him to show us anything in our hearts or minds that needs to be pruned or removed, and ask God to give us the strength to conquer whatever it is that isn't lovely.

ACTIVITY #1: STAY CONNECTED TO THE VINE

Pick a spiritual practice to do every day this week to stay connected to Jesus. You might choose praying, studying your Bible, singing worship songs, sitting still to listen for God, taking a walk daily to observe God's creation, drawing or painting in response to God in your life, journaling, or memorizing a Bible verse. You can also search online for "spiritual disciplines" to discover other ways you can connect with God. (Parents, two great resources for your own spiritual development are *Celebration of Discipline* by Richard J. Foster and *Spiritual Disciplines Handbook* by Adele Ahlberg Calhoun.)

ACTIVITY #2: FRUIT BASKET

Bear much fruit! Prepare a basket of fresh fruit to deliver to someone in need, a local homeless shelter, or other ministry that serves people in your community.

The Science of Pruning

Vineyard owners, farmers, botanists, arborists, and horticulturalists will quickly understand the metaphor of the vine and the branches, but if you aren't someone who grows plants or trees, the idea of pruning in order to bear more fruit can seem strange. Why would you trim a plant if you want it to grow?

Plants use a lot of energy to try to heal an injured or diseased branch. Even though cutting off that branch is also a form of injury, it allows the plant's energy to go toward new, healthier growth. In the case of grapevines, grapes only grow on one-year-old wood, so in order to produce more grapes each year, the grape grower must selectively and artfully prune away some old and unfruitful branches to help the vine produce bunches of fresh grapes each year.

Change Is on the Way

SETTING UP THE STORY

Jesus continued to prepare the disciples for what they would experience next, knowing that it would change the world. True to form, the disciples were confused and unsure of what Jesus was trying to say to them. Learning from a teacher who is upending your understanding of religion is challenging! Jesus knew the disciples' struggles and continued to guide and direct them, all the way through his arrest, death, and resurrection.

READ: JOHN 16:16–33 (NIV)

Jesus went on to say, "In a little while you will see me no more, and then after a little while you will see me."

At this, some of his disciples said to one another, "What does he mean by saying, 'In a little while you will see me no more, and then after a little while you will see me,' and 'Because I am going to the Father'?" They kept asking, "What does he mean by 'a little while'? We don't understand what he is saying."

Jesus saw that they wanted to ask him about this, so he said to them, "Are you asking one another what I meant when I said, 'In a little while you will see me no more, and then after a little while you will see me'? Very truly I tell you, you will weep and mourn while the world rejoices. You will grieve, but your grief will turn to joy. A woman giving birth to a child has pain because her time has come; but when her baby is born she forgets the anguish because of her joy that a child is born into the world. So with you: Now is your time of grief, but I will see you again and you will rejoice, and no one will take away your joy. In that day you will no longer ask me anything. Very truly I tell you, my Father will give you whatever you ask in my name. Until now you have not asked for anything in my name. Ask and you will receive, and your joy will be complete.

"Though I have been speaking figuratively, a time is coming when I will no longer use this kind of language but will tell you plainly about my Father. In that day you will ask in my name. I am not saying that I will ask the Father on your behalf. No, the Father himself loves you because you have loved me and have believed that I came from God. I came from the Father and entered the world; now I am leaving the world and going back to the Father."

Then Jesus' disciples said, "Now you are speaking clearly and without figures of speech. Now we can see that you know all things and that you do not even need to have anyone ask you questions. This makes us believe that you came from God."

"Do you now believe?" Jesus replied. "A time is coming and in fact has come when you will be scattered, each to your own home. You will leave me all alone. Yet I am not alone, for my Father is with me.

"I have told you these things, so that in me you may have peace. In this world you will have trouble. But take heart! I have overcome the world."

TALK ABOUT IT

- What did Jesus mean when he said, "In a little while you will see me no more, and then after a little while you will see me"?
- What are some things in your life that were hard or painful for a little while, but then when it was over, there was celebration?
- Parents, share your child's birth story with them. If your child is a foster child or was adopted, describe the journey to joining your family. Was it hard? Were you afraid? What was it like after they arrived?
- What makes you trust a person, what they say or how they act?
- How does Jesus's final words in today's story make you feel?
- Is there anything that confuses you about this story? If so, it's okay! Let's talk about it.
- Do you have any questions about John 16:16–33?

CLOSING THOUGHT

In his final moments with the disciples, Jesus explained his relationship with the Father (God) and how that relationship should comfort them.

Before Jesus came, only the priests, the holiest people, could access God. Priests performed the acts of worship and sacrifice to intercede with God on behalf of the people. An intercessor, or mediator, works between two groups to try to smooth things over when their relationship is broken. That was the role of the priest—when the people of God broke their end of their relationship with God (called a covenant), the priests would perform sacrifices to try to restore the people to God.

Jesus put an end to all those sacrifices. He showed his followers that the true way of the Father is the same way of the Son; they are one and the same. The only person you need to be able to access God's love is God's Son, Jesus. Because of your trust in Jesus, you can connect with God yourself, anytime. Jesus says you can ask God for anything in his name. No matter what happens, no matter what trouble, you can have peace because Jesus has overcome the world!

PRAYER PROMPT

Jesus, thank you for showing us the way to the Father. Thank you for opening the door for us to enter into God's presence ourselves, to know your great love and acceptance for us, and to find your peace and joy no matter what happens in the world. Thank you for knowing what we're worried about before we even speak. Help us to remember that we can turn to you anytime, and you will be there to comfort us and bring us peace.

ACTIVITY #1: TAKE HEART!

Write a note for someone who is going through a tragedy or crisis right now to encourage them. Make a point of praying for that person this week (this is called intercessory prayer), and try to remember to check in on them regularly as a way to extend God's love to them.

ACTIVITY #2: PLAY THE MIDDLE MAN

Jesus told the disciples that a time was coming when they wouldn't need to first ask Jesus for something, and then have Jesus ask God on their behalf. They would be able to go directly to God himself. Play a game of Simon Says with your family, only whoever is Simon should whisper commands into another person's ear. Then the "Middle Man" should give the command on behalf of Simon. Take turns being the Middle Man. For an even sillier version, play a game of Telephone, where one person whispers a message in another person's ear, and that person passes the message along to the next, and so on, until everyone has heard the message. What crazy ways did the message change?

The Pains of Childbirth

Jesus spent a lot of time right before his death and resurrection trying to prepare the disciples for what they were about to experience. The imagery he used in today's story comes out of stories the disciples already knew. The Old Testament prophets used the analogy of childbirth to explain the coming act of salvation: it would be painful and hard but would result in great joy. For years, the Jewish people had been longing for the arrival of their Messiah and the coming salvation. Jesus used these familiar terms and language to help the disciples understand that what they were experiencing in those final days and in the days to come was the fulfillment of those hopes: the Messiah is here, and he is Jesus!

Jesus's Prayer for His Followers

SETTING UP THE STORY

Jesus finished his last evening with the disciples before his arrest praying over them. There's a lot of encouraging and important thoughts from our Savior in this story; let's hear the words Jesus prayed for the disciples (and prayed for us as well!).

READ: JOHN 17 (NLT)

After saying all these things, Jesus looked up to heaven and said, "Father, the hour has come. Glorify your Son so he can give glory back to you. For you have given him authority over everyone. He gives eternal life to each one you have given him. And this is the way to have eternal life—to know you, the only true God, and Jesus Christ, the one you sent to earth. I brought glory to you here on earth by completing the work you gave me to do. Now, Father, bring me into the glory we shared before the world began.

"I have revealed you to the ones you gave me from this world. They were always yours. You gave them to me, and they have kept your word. Now they know that everything I have is a gift from you, for I have passed on to them the message you gave me. They accepted it and know that I came from you, and they believe you sent me.

"My prayer is not for the world, but for those you have given me, because they belong to you. All who are mine belong to you, and you have given them to me, so they bring me glory. Now I am departing from the world; they are staying in this world, but I am coming to you. Holy Father, you have given me your name; now protect them by the power of your name so that they will be united just as we are. During my time here, I protected them by the power of the name you gave me. I guarded them so that not one was lost, except the one headed for destruction, as the Scriptures foretold.

"Now I am coming to you. I told them many things while I was with them in this world so they would be filled with my joy. I have given them your word. And the world hates them because they do not belong to the world, just as I do not belong to the world. I'm not asking you to take them out of the world, but to keep them safe from the evil one. They do not belong to this world any more than I do. Make them holy by your truth; teach them your word, which is truth. Just as you sent me into the world, I am sending them into the world. And I give myself as a holy sacrifice for them so they can be made holy by your truth.

"I am praying not only for these disciples but also for all who will ever believe in me through their message. I pray that they will all be one, just as you and I are one—as you are in me, Father, and I am in you. And may they be in us so that the world will believe you sent me.

"I have given them the glory you gave me, so they may be one as we are one. I am in them and you are in me. May they experience such perfect unity that the world will know that you sent me and that you love them as much as you love me. Father, I want these whom you have given me to be with me where I am. Then they can see all the glory you gave me because you loved me even before the world began!

"O righteous Father, the world doesn't know you, but I do; and these disciples know you sent me. I have revealed you to them, and I will continue to do so. Then your love for me will be in them, and I will be in them."

TALK ABOUT IT

- How does it make you feel to know that you belong to God?
- Did Jesus ask God to take us out of the world? What was his prayer?
- What do you think it means that Jesus and his followers do not belong to this world?
- Why do you think Jesus chose this moment before his arrest to pray for unity among his followers?

- Have you ever had someone pray for you when you were in their presence? How did it make you feel?
- Is there anything that confuses you about this story? If so, it's okay! Let's talk about it.
- Do you have any questions about John 17?

CLOSING THOUGHT

Jesus prayed for the disciples who were with him and for every follower of Jesus Christ who would come later, even us! He prayed that we would know we belong to the Father. He prayed that God would protect us from the bad things in the world. He prayed that we would be united with other believers in God's love, so that we could be at peace with each other and so that the world would know we are God's children. Our unity as followers of Christ is a great demonstration of God's love to the rest of the world, who don't know Jesus yet.

On the brink of Jesus's arrest, he knew that the disciples listening would desert him, and yet still he prayed for their unity. Jesus has a perfect hope for his followers. He wants us to know God's love, to know we are part of God's family, and to be of the same mind with other believers, pursuing God's truth and showing his love to the rest of the hurting world. What a powerful prayer!

PRAYER PROMPT

Let's thank God for all of the people in the world who call Jesus their Savior. Let's ask God to unify the church around the globe and to give us courage to love others in his name. Ask God to help your family be united with other believers, even when they worship differently or have different ideas about how to live as Christians.

ACTIVITY #1: CHURCH VISIT

Go on a Sunday morning adventure and attend a church that is a different denomination than your own. What was the same? What was different? What did God teach you through the experience?

ACTIVITY #2: BE UNITED

Invite a family from a different church tradition over for a meal. Ask them in advance if it's okay to talk about religion. Ask them what their tradition believes that is unique to them, and share with your friends what is unique about your tradition. At the end of your time together, take turns praying for one another, that you might be unified in Christ.

Denominations of Christianity

Jesus prayed for unity among the believers, but almost immediately after he ascended into heaven, divisions began. Throughout history, Christians have formed different groups. These groups have most recently been called denominations. Denominations are organizations of Christians who believe in Jesus Christ but have a particular view on how to live out their faith. The differences could be about worship, the Bible, how we take Communion, or ways to practice our faith. There are many, many denominations; in fact, according to the *World Christian Encyclopedia Online*, there were 33,830 denominations worldwide in 2001,[10] and that number has probably grown since. Despite our differences, we worship the same God and are called to be unified and to love one another.

Section 3

PETER AND JESUS

You Are Who You Say You Are

SETTING UP THE STORY

We've read many stories of unlikely disciples who sought out and followed Jesus, and how Jesus interacted with those disciples. We've also read stories about how Jesus talked with and taught the twelve disciples. Now we're going to focus on one of the disciples closest to Jesus: Peter. We can learn a lot about Jesus—how he related to his closest friends and how we should interact with our friends—through the stories shared about Peter and Jesus.

READ: LUKE 9:18–27 (MSG)

One time when Jesus was off praying by himself, his disciples nearby, he asked them, "What are the crowds saying about me, about who I am?"

They said, "John the Baptizer. Others say Elijah. Still others say that one of the prophets from long ago has come back."

He then asked, "And you—what are you saying about me? Who am I?"

Peter answered, "The Messiah of God." Jesus then warned them to keep it quiet. They were to tell no one what Peter had said.

He went on, "It is necessary that the Son of Man proceed to an ordeal of suffering, be tried and found guilty by the religious leaders, high priests, and religion scholars, be killed, and on the third day be raised up alive."

Then he told them what they could expect for themselves: "Anyone who intends to come with me has to let me lead. You're not in the driver's seat—I am. Don't run from suffering; embrace it. Follow me and I'll show you how. Self-help is no help at all. Self-sacrifice is the way, *my* way, to finding yourself, your true self. What good would it do to get everything you want and lose you, the real you? If any of you is embarrassed with me and the way I'm leading you, know that the Son of Man will be far more embarrassed with you when he arrives in all his splendor in company with the Father and the holy angels. This isn't, you realize, pie in the sky by and by. Some who have taken their stand right here are going to see it happen, see with their own eyes the kingdom of God."

TALK ABOUT IT

- Have you ever felt like people don't know the real you? How does that make you feel?
- Who does Peter say Jesus is?
- What did Jesus tell the disciples they should expect as his followers?
- What do you think Jesus meant when he said, "What good would it do to get everything you want and lose you, the real you"?
- What is something about you that makes you "the real you"?
- Is there anything that confuses you about this story? If so, it's okay! Let's talk about it.
- Do you have any questions about Luke 9:18–27?

CLOSING THOUGHT

Peter was the first of the apostles to call Jesus the Messiah, or promised savior, of the Jewish nation. As the Messiah, Jesus came to rescue the Jewish people (and all people), but what the people had in mind looked very different from reality. The Jews and disciples expected a warrior who would lead them in victory to reign over all other nations, but Jesus warned the disciples that they were in for a more difficult road—one of suffering instead of conquering.

In the midst of explaining more about what following Jesus looked like, Jesus told his disciples that self-sacrifice is the way to finding your true self. The heart of self-sacrifice is loving others, and Jesus demonstrated that love all the way to the cross and beyond.

The people closest to Jesus knew him—the real him—best. When you have a friendship built on love, you can be the real you with that person, unafraid of judgment or rejection.

Even though Jesus wasn't the Messiah they expected, he was the friend they needed.

PRAYER PROMPT

Lord, it is hard sometimes to follow in your footsteps and let you lead us. Even though we want to do things our way to get what we think will bring about our happiness, your way requires self-sacrifice. When we follow you, even though it can be hard, the reward of acting out of love is always great. Please help us to surrender our own will and let yours be done, every day.

ACTIVITY #1: THE REAL YOU

Share with each other one character trait you see in each of your family members that you think defines who they really are.

ACTIVITY #2: FRIEND CONFESSION

Choose one friend to write or call, just to tell them some things you love about them that make them special. It isn't about what they've done or what they've accomplished, but who they *are*.

The Long-Awaited Messiah

As Christians, we identify Jesus as the true Messiah, but during Jesus's time, there were many figures who were thought to be the messiah of the Jewish nation. After centuries of living under the rule of other nations, the Jews hoped and believed God would send a Savior who would end all of their suffering and establish the Jewish kingdom again. Many believed he would be powerful and strong, a mighty warrior. Instead, Jesus came as a humble servant, bringing peace, restoring relationships, and ministering to the oppressed. His mission looked a lot different, and that was hard for many to swallow, even his closest disciples!

Following Jesus, Even When It's Hard

SETTING UP THE STORY

(If you have time, it might help to read the full chapter of John 6 for today's devotional.) After Jesus performed two famous miracles, the crowd wanted Jesus to tell them what they had to do to follow God. Jesus said they needed to believe in the one whom God sent. Then Jesus said, "I am the living bread that came down from heaven. Whoever eats this bread will live forever. This bread is my flesh, which I will give for the life of the world" (John 6:51 NIV). Eat a man's flesh? The followers didn't know what to make of that!

READ: JOHN 6:60–71 (NIV)

On hearing it, many of his disciples said, "This is a hard teaching. Who can accept it?"

Aware that his disciples were grumbling about this, Jesus said to them, "Does this offend you? Then what if you see the Son of Man ascend to where he was before! The Spirit gives life; the flesh counts for nothing. The words I have spoken to you—they are full of the Spirit and life. Yet there are some of you who do not believe." For Jesus had known from the beginning which of them did not believe and who would betray him. He went on to say, "This is why I told you that no one can come to me unless the Father has enabled them."

From this time many of his disciples turned back and no longer followed him.

"You do not want to leave too, do you?" Jesus asked the Twelve.

Simon Peter answered him, "Lord, to whom shall we go? You have the words of eternal life. We have come to believe and to know that you are the Holy One of God."

Then Jesus replied, "Have I not chosen you, the Twelve? Yet one of you is a devil!" (He meant Judas, the son of Simon Iscariot, who, though one of the Twelve, was later to betray him.)

TALK ABOUT IT

- How did many of the disciples react to Jesus's hard words about believing that he is the bread of life, the one God sent, the Son of God?
- Have you ever felt out of place because you believed something different from your friends? How did that feel?
- How do you think Jesus felt when many of the disciples turned back and no longer followed him?
- Have you ever found it hard to follow Jesus? Can you share an example?
- Why do you think Jesus let Judas Iscariot stay with the disciples, even though Jesus knew that Judas would betray him later?
- Is there anything that confuses you about this story? If so, it's okay! Let's talk about it.
- Do you have any questions about John 6:60–71?

CLOSING THOUGHT

The more we dig into Jesus's words, the more his words challenge us. Hebrews 4:12 says, "The word of God is alive and active. Sharper than any double-edged sword, it penetrates even to dividing soul and spirit, joints and marrow; it judges the thoughts and attitudes of the heart" (NIV).

The crowd who watched Jesus feed five thousand men plus their families were amazed and wanted to know more about how they could get closer to God. But when Jesus started to say hard things about God and himself, many of the disciples found it too hard and turned away.

When Jesus asked the disciples whether they wanted to leave him too, Simon Peter raised his voice and declared his allegiance to Jesus as the Son of God. It takes courage and strength to stay true to what you believe when your beliefs are challenged.

Stick to Jesus, the author and perfecter of your faith. He showed us what it means to love God and love others. Sometimes the hard teaching is exactly what we need to become more mature followers of Christ.

PRAYER PROMPT

As we read God's Word, sometimes we'll encounter passages of Scripture that are hard for us to accept. Let's ask God to soften our hearts to receive his teaching. Let's pray together these words from Psalm 119:97–98 (NIV):

> Oh, how I love your law!
> I meditate on it all day long.
> Your commands are always with me
> and make me wiser than my enemies.

ACTIVITY #1: A FAITHFUL FRIEND

Think about someone who has been a faithful friend to your family, like Simon Peter was to Jesus in today's story. If they live nearby, consider having them over for a meal. If they live far away, plan some way to thank them for always being there for your family.

ACTIVITY #2: MEDITATE ON A VERSE

When we memorize Scripture, it lives with us and helps to guide us. Choose a verse from today's reading to memorize this week. You might choose John 6:35; Hebrews 4:12; Psalm 119:97–98; or a different verse that is important to your family right now.

Judas Iscariot and Simon Peter

Both Simon Peter and Judas Iscariot were counted as two of Jesus's closest disciples, the "Twelve." Simon Peter along with James and John were closest to Jesus during his ministry, while Judas is often only mentioned in contrast or to foreshadow the coming betrayal. Both disciples were given the opportunity to leave Jesus's ministry in today's story, but both stay, even though later Judas betrayed Jesus, and Simon Peter denied knowing Jesus. God knew the makeup of both men's hearts and still welcomed them into his midst. Their stories show us just how true it is that the only way to God is through believing in the Son, Jesus Christ, and the love he demonstrated for all humankind.

Meeting with Moses and Elijah on the Mountain

SETTING UP THE STORY

As one of Jesus's closest disciples, Peter got to witness lots of miracles—healings and the multiplication of food, turning water into wine, raising people from the dead, and more. In today's story, Peter and a couple of the other disciples watch as two heroes of the Old Testament defy space and time to talk with Jesus! This is a mountaintop encounter like never before.

READ: LUKE 9:28–36 (NLT)

About eight days later Jesus took Peter, John, and James up on a mountain to pray. And as he was praying, the appearance of his face was transformed, and his clothes became dazzling white. Suddenly, two men, Moses and Elijah, appeared and began talking with Jesus. They were glorious to see. And they were speaking about his exodus from this world, which was about to be fulfilled in Jerusalem.

Peter and the others had fallen asleep. When they woke up, they saw Jesus' glory and the two men standing with him. As Moses and Elijah were starting to leave, Peter, not even knowing what he was saying, blurted out, "Master, it's wonderful for us to be here! Let's make three shelters as memorials—one for you, one for Moses, and one for Elijah." But even as he was saying this, a cloud overshadowed them, and terror gripped them as the cloud covered them.

Then a voice from the cloud said, "This is my Son, my Chosen One. Listen to him." When the voice finished, Jesus was there alone. They didn't tell anyone at that time what they had seen.

TALK ABOUT IT

- Why did Jesus and the disciples go up the mountain?
- If two famous people from history reappeared and started talking to you, how would you react?
- If you could choose two people from any time in history to come back and have a conversation with, who would you pick?
- Why do you think Peter wanted to build a shelter for the three men?
- Why do you think the disciples didn't tell anyone about what happened with Jesus, Moses, and Elijah on the mountain?
- Is there anything that confuses you about this story? If so, it's okay! Let's talk about it.
- Do you have any questions about Luke 9:28–36?

CLOSING THOUGHT

Eight days earlier Peter had said he believed Jesus was the Messiah sent from God. This trip up the mountain was like God giving Peter two thumbs up on that belief: *Yes! This is my Son! Listen to him!*

Jesus brought the disciples up the mountain to pray. When Jesus went off to pray, he didn't just talk to God, he listened for God. He found himself surrounded by the presence of God's Spirit. Not only was God's Spirit present, along came two heroes of the Jewish faith, Moses and Elijah!

Peter didn't know what to do at that moment. The truth is, he didn't need to do anything, just sit and be in God's presence alongside Jesus. Peter wanted to respond to the glory of God around him by building something to memorialize the spot. But the last thing Jesus, Moses, and Elijah needed were monuments. Instead, the voice of God called from within the cloud surrounding them, *Pay attention to my Son, whom I love. What he says to you is truth and life. Do as he says!*

PRAYER PROMPT

When you pray together today, set aside attempts to impress God with choosing the right words and just enjoy being in the presence of God. Ask God to open your ears so you can listen and do what he wants you to do.

ACTIVITY #1: ACTIVE LISTENING

Sometimes we need to sit still in order to hear from God. After you ask God to help you listen, sit together in silence for a minute or two. While you are still, try to focus only on God. When time is up, share what, if anything, you saw, felt, thought, or heard inside during that quiet moment. If you didn't experience anything, that's okay! Try again together as a family or by yourself another time as a way to calm your spirit and grow closer to God.

ACTIVITY #2: LOOK CLOSER

Go to a nearby park, woods, or nature center. Find a spot under a tree, near a rock, or next to some water and see what you can find. Stoop low and look at rocks, insects, and leaves. God's design is in everything! Take pictures of new wonders you've discovered.

Moses and Elijah

Jesus often said that he came to fulfill what was said about him in the law and the prophets. When Moses and Elijah appear with Jesus on top of the mountain, they are more than just two important figures from the Old Testament. Moses brought the Ten Commandments, or the law, down from his encounter with God on the mountain and taught it to the Israelites. Elijah was one of God's prophets, who defended the worship of the Hebrew God over the Canaanites' god, Baal. God also performed many miracles through Elijah, including resurrection. Moses's and Elijah's appearance with Jesus points to Jesus's fulfillment of all that was said by the law (Moses) and the prophets (Elijah) in the Scriptures.

What the Master Does,
You Should Do as Well

SETTING UP THE STORY

Peter saw Jesus in all his glory on top of a mountain. He called Jesus the promised Messiah of God. He watched Jesus perform miracle after miracle. But Jesus must have known Peter didn't quite understand yet what he was supposed to take away from all of the lessons Jesus had taught during his three years of ministry. Right up until his crucifixion, Jesus had still more things he wanted to make sure his disciples—and us—grasped about who Jesus was and how we're supposed to live as his followers.

READ: JOHN 13:1–17 (MSG)

Just before the Passover Feast, Jesus knew that the time had come to leave this world to go to the Father. Having loved his dear companions, he continued to love them right to the end. It was suppertime. The Devil by now had Judas, son of Simon the Iscariot, firmly in his grip, all set for the betrayal.

Jesus knew that the Father had put him in complete charge of everything, that he came from God and was on his way back to God. So he got up from the supper table, set aside his robe, and put on an apron. Then he poured water into a basin and began to wash the feet of the disciples, drying them with his apron. When he got to Simon Peter, Peter said, "Master, *you* wash *my* feet?"

Jesus answered, "You don't understand now what I'm doing, but it will be clear enough to you later."

Peter persisted, "You're not going to wash my feet—ever!"

Jesus said, "If I don't wash you, you can't be part of what I'm doing."

"Master!" said Peter. "Not only my feet, then. Wash my hands! Wash my head!"

Jesus said, "If you've had a bath in the morning, you only need your feet washed now and you're clean from head to toe. My concern, you understand, is holiness, not hygiene. So now you're clean. But not every one of you." (He knew who was betraying him. That's why he said, "Not every one of you.") After he had finished washing their feet, he took his robe, put it back on, and went back to his place at the table.

Then he said, "Do you understand what I have done to you? You address me as 'Teacher' and 'Master,' and rightly so. That is what I am. So if I, the Master and Teacher, washed your feet, you must now wash each other's feet. I've laid down a pattern for you. What I've done, you do. I'm only pointing out the obvious. A servant is not ranked above his master; an employee doesn't give orders to the employer. If you understand what I'm telling you, act like it—and live a blessed life."

TALK ABOUT IT
- How do you expect people with power to act?
- How would you feel if someone suddenly started washing your feet?
- What was Peter's reaction to Jesus washing his feet?
- Have you ever had someone do something for you that was above and beyond what you would ever have expected? How did it make you feel?
- What does Jesus expect from his disciples, based on today's story?
- Is there anything that confuses you about this story? If so, it's okay! Let's talk about it.
- Do you have any questions about John 13:1–17?

CLOSING THOUGHT
There are lots of people in power who *love* being in power. They would never even think about stooping down to wash their followers' feet. Those kinds of behaviors are beneath them. The disciples would have been used to that kind of a ruler. So when Jesus took off his robe and began washing

Peter's feet, Peter was shocked. The Son of God lowering himself to the position of a servant? Peter even protested against it!

But Jesus wanted to show Peter what real power looked like.

Jesus was always modeling a different way of leading, living, and loving to his disciples. Even when Peter didn't understand what Jesus was doing, Jesus was patient with him. He continued to model and explain what being a disciple of God looked like . . . and it looked a whole lot different from what the disciples had seen from other religious leaders. It looked like laying down your life for your friends. It looked like serving instead of ruling. It looked like love.

PRAYER PROMPT

It's in our human nature to want power and control, but Jesus modeled service and love instead. Let's thank God for the example of Jesus and ask him to help us value others above ourselves.

ACTIVITY #1: PEDICURE TIME!

Follow Jesus's example from today and wash each other's feet. You'll need a little bucket or basin, some towels, and some warm water. Pray for the person whose feet you are washing to live a blessed life.

ACTIVITY #2: SERVICE PROJECT

Ask a neighbor or elderly relative if there are any chores around their home you could do for them.

Why Feet Washing?

Washing your hands and feet in the Old Testament was a symbol of purity and sinlessness. Priests were not allowed to enter the temple until they had washed their hands and feet. It was also a matter of basic hygiene, just like today. Imagine taking a long walk barefoot. How dirty would your feet be, even after just a short time outside? The same was true in Jesus's time. During biblical times, it was also a sign of hospitality to have someone wash your feet when you arrived. Normally, a servant would be given the job of washing a person's feet, but certainly not the ruler or master of the house. Not only does the foot washing symbolize the way Jesus cleanses us of our sins, but it also models true leadership as a selfless act of love.

Jesus's New Command to the Guys in the Upper Room

SETTING UP THE STORY

The time that the disciples spent in the upper room before Jesus was arrested was a special time with him and his closest friends. There was a lot Jesus taught his disciples during that Passover Feast. After Jesus dismissed Judas from the room, he continued to share with the disciples a message from the heart about what he expected from them—and from us, the followers of Jesus who read these stories today.

READ: JOHN 13:31–38 (NIV)

When he was gone, Jesus said, "Now the Son of Man is glorified and God is glorified in him. If God is glorified in him, God will glorify the Son in himself, and will glorify him at once.

"My children, I will be with you only a little longer. You will look for me, and just as I told the Jews, so I tell you now: Where I am going, you cannot come.

"A new command I give you: Love one another. As I have loved you, so you must love one another. By this everyone will know that you are my disciples, if you love one another."

Simon Peter asked him, "Lord, where are you going?"

Jesus replied, "Where I am going, you cannot follow now, but you will follow later."

Peter asked, "Lord, why can't I follow you now? I will lay down my life for you."

Then Jesus answered, "Will you really lay down your life for me? Very truly I tell you, before the rooster crows, you will disown me three times!"

TALK ABOUT IT

- Where do you think Jesus was going?
- What is the sign that we are disciples of Jesus?
- How do you think Peter felt when Jesus told him that Peter would disown him?
- How do you feel when you have been betrayed?
- Why do you think the command to love one another is so hard to follow, even though it sounds so simple?
- Is there anything that confuses you about this story? If so, it's okay! Let's talk about it.
- Do you have any questions about John 13:31–38?

CLOSING THOUGHT

Sitting in the upper room during Passover, Jesus knew everything that was coming. He knew Judas was on his way to turn him over to the Pharisees. He knew Peter would deny knowing him after his arrest. He knew he was headed for the cross.

He also knew that on the other side of the cross was resurrection and life.

Peter and the other disciples couldn't know those things, even though Jesus kept telling them what was about to happen. They couldn't comprehend why Jesus would go somewhere without them. Peter believed and confessed that Jesus was the Son of God, and when Jesus said he needed to leave them, Peter truly believed he would never leave Jesus's side.

Jesus knew Peter's heart, his passion and desire to please his Lord, and he knew Peter's lingering fear. He had seen that fear when he asked Peter to walk on the water to him. There was more work to be done.

The Son of God is compassionate, merciful, and patient with his followers, even as they stumble over themselves. Jesus keeps working on our hearts until it's time to meet him face-to-face in heaven.

PRAYER PROMPT

Let's praise God for his constant love, patience, and mercy, and thank him for how patient he is with us. Ask him to show us every day how we can love one another the way Jesus loves us.

ACTIVITY #1: STEP ONE: LOVE

Loving one another feels really big, but it's super simple when you break it down into small steps. What's one way you tend to be self-serving or selfish? Surrender that to God and promise each other that you will work on that one thing this week. Whenever you are tempted to do that thing, invite God in and pray for the same patience, kindness, and self-control God has toward each of us, and act out of love instead.

ACTIVITY #2: MEMORY VERSE

Jesus's new command to love one another is the heart of this devotional. Let's memorize John 13:34 (NIV) this week: "A new command I give you: Love one another. As I have loved you, so you must love one another." Write the verse on a poster and hang it on your wall or fridge as a reminder of what God calls you to do.

God's Patience with Peter

It is wonderful that Jesus is so patient with us, but *why* is he so patient? Wouldn't it have been better to have a band of strong and powerful disciples ready to take over for Jesus after he was gone? Even though we might appreciate it, God's patience is hard for us to understand. Long after Jesus died and rose from the dead, Peter wrote a couple of letters to encourage other believers. After all of the ways Peter stumbled trying to be the perfect follower, he had learned a thing or two about God's patience. In one of his letters, Peter wrote, "The Lord is not slow in keeping his promise, as some understand slowness. Instead he is patient with you, not wanting anyone to perish, but everyone to come to repentance" (2 Peter 3:9 NIV). That's the kind of love God has for us, the kind of love that never gives up on us.

Jesus and the Sleepy Disciples in the Garden of Gethsemane

SETTING UP THE STORY

After the Passover dinner, the disciples followed Jesus into a garden where he went to pray. This was a dark night for Jesus, who knew that Judas was on his way with a crowd armed with weapons sent by the chief priests and Pharisees to arrest him. Let's see how Jesus managed this time with Peter and some of the other disciples by his side.

READ: MATTHEW 26:36–46 (NLT)

Then Jesus went with them to the olive grove called Gethsemane, and he said, "Sit here while I go over there to pray." He took Peter and Zebedee's two sons, James and John, and he became anguished and distressed. He told them, "My soul is crushed with grief to the point of death. Stay here and keep watch with me."

He went on a little farther and bowed with his face to the ground, praying, "My Father! If it is possible, let this cup of suffering be taken away from me. Yet I want your will to be done, not mine."

Then he returned to the disciples and found them asleep. He said to Peter, "Couldn't you watch with me even one hour? Keep watch and pray, so that you will not give in to temptation. For the spirit is willing, but the body is weak!"

Then Jesus left them a second time and prayed, "My Father! If this cup cannot be taken away unless I drink it, your will be done." When he returned to them again, he found them sleeping, for they couldn't keep their eyes open.

So he went to pray a third time, saying the same things again. Then he came to the disciples and said, "Go ahead and sleep. Have your rest. But look—the time has come. The Son of Man is betrayed into the hands of sinners. Up, let's be going. Look, my betrayer is here!"

TALK ABOUT IT

- What do you think Jesus meant when he asked God to take away the "cup of suffering"?
- How was Jesus feeling during this moment?
- What happened to the disciples while Jesus was praying?
- Why do you think Jesus was upset that the disciples kept falling asleep?
- Why do you think Jesus went away to pray to God three times?
- Is there anything that confuses you about this story? If so, it's okay! Let's talk about it.
- Do you have any questions about Matthew 26:36–46?

CLOSING THOUGHT

Jesus knew what was coming to him—Judas was on his way to betray him. He knew the suffering that awaited him on the cross. In the garden before the betrayal, Jesus asked if there might be any other way.

Because he had free will just like the rest of us, Jesus could have run away from the unfair punishment that awaited him on the cross. He asked God three times for some other way. Each time he rose off of his knees with strength and determination to face what came next. The hope and the promise of God's great love pushed Jesus onward to accomplish the mission.

Even Peter, one of Jesus's closest disciples, struggled to keep watch and stay awake during Jesus's time of distress. When all others fall away, God the Father remains close to the brokenhearted, and the Holy Spirit remains the Comforter. We can learn from Jesus both how to go to God in prayer in our moment of need and how to persevere through suffering with our hope in God our Savior, even if all others leave our side.

PRAYER PROMPT

When we are stressed or upset about something that is happening, we can take that trouble to the Lord in prayer. What is something you are worried about? Let's follow Jesus's example and ask God for what we hope will happen, while not forgetting to pray for his will to be done. Ask God for the same strength and determination he gave Jesus to persevere through whatever trouble we face in life.

ACTIVITY #1: PRAYING POSITIONS

There are many different positions—or postures—you can take when you pray. Some people kneel. Some stand and raise their hands to the sky. Some bow their heads and fold their hands. In today's story, Jesus got down on his knees and bowed his head close to the ground. There's no right or wrong posture when it comes to prayer. This week, try taking a different posture when you pray. Have fun with it! Talk with your family about your experience.

ACTIVITY #2: EATING WITH OLIVES OR OLIVE OIL

The garden of Gethsemane was an olive grove that sat at the foot of the Mount of Olives.[1] Olives and olive oil are symbols of joy and gladness.[2] It's hard to imagine Jesus experienced any kind of joy at this moment, but Hebrews 12:2 says, "Because of the joy awaiting him, he endured the cross" (NLT). Even though much of our lesson has talked about grief and sadness, God promises joy in the morning! Together with your family, prepare a meal that uses olives or olive oil. As you enjoy the food, share with each other stories of times that have been very hard but how God brought joy through that challenge.

The Garden of Gethsemane

The word *Gethsemane* means "oil press."[3] Olives, olive trees, and olive branches carry a lot of significance in Scripture. The first time olives are mentioned in the Bible, a dove carried an olive branch back to Noah after the flood as a sign that the water had retreated. Olives and olive branches are symbols of peace and reconciliation throughout the world. Psalm 52:8 says, "But I am like an olive tree, thriving in the house of God. I will always trust in God's unfailing love" (NLT). There within the olive grove, Jesus accepted his mission to reconcile all things to God and bring peace to his people.

Jesus and the Way of Suffering

SETTING UP THE STORY

Jesus continued to model what it means for us to love one another all the way up to the cross and after his resurrection. As Jesus got up off his knees from praying for the third time in the garden of Gethsemane, he prepared to meet the crowd that was on its way to arrest him. Peter had an idea about what should be done in that moment; let's see what Jesus thought about his approach.

READ: JOHN 18:1–11 (NLT)

After saying these things, Jesus crossed the Kidron Valley with his disciples and entered a grove of olive trees. Judas, the betrayer, knew this place, because Jesus had often gone there with his disciples. The leading priests and Pharisees had given Judas a contingent of Roman soldiers and Temple guards to accompany him. Now with blazing torches, lanterns, and weapons, they arrived at the olive grove.

Jesus fully realized all that was going to happen to him, so he stepped forward to meet them. "Who are you looking for?" he asked.

"Jesus the Nazarene," they replied.

"I AM he," Jesus said. (Judas, who betrayed him, was standing with them.) As Jesus said "I AM he," they all drew back and fell to the ground! Once more he asked them, "Who are you looking for?"

And again they replied, "Jesus the Nazarene."

"I told you that I AM he," Jesus said. "And since I am the one you want, let these others go." He did this to fulfill his own statement: "I did not lose a single one of those you have given me."

Then Simon Peter drew a sword and slashed off the right ear of Malchus, the high priest's slave. But Jesus said to Peter, "Put your sword back into its sheath. Shall I not drink from the cup of suffering the Father has given me?"

TALK ABOUT IT

- Who were all the people involved in arresting Jesus?
- Why do you think the crowd of soldiers and temple guards fell to the ground when Jesus said, "I AM he"?
- Try to imagine what it was like to be by Jesus's side in the garden. How do you think you would feel?
- Why do you think Jesus told Peter to put away his sword?
- Is there anything that confuses you about this story? If so, it's okay! Let's talk about it.
- Do you have any questions about John 18:1–11?

CLOSING THOUGHT

Like Peter, we all want to defend the people we love the most so they don't have to suffer. Jesus had a different way of handling the situation and different thoughts about suffering. No one wants to suffer, and yet Jesus scolded Peter for trying to protect and defend him. Jesus knew God was not going to keep him from the cross—he just prayed in the garden about it. Jesus knew something Peter hadn't fully grasped: When we go through challenging times, they are often used by God to develop perseverance, sharpen character, and renew hope.

Jesus showed the disciples a different way of dealing with those who threaten us, a way of peace and nonviolence. Jesus didn't fight back. He didn't let his disciples fight for him. Jesus's response to Peter shows us that our loyalty to our friends and family still needs to be overshadowed by love, even for those who threaten us. That's hard to do!

With Christ, all things are possible. We can do hard things.

PRAYER PROMPT

If you are suffering right now, or know someone who is, pray for God's strength and courage to weather the storm, knowing that God can bring hope even through their suffering. Ask God to help you surrender your loyalties in order to seek the higher truth of God's love.

ACTIVITY #1: PETER AND THE SWORD

Act out with your family members the scene in the garden with the soldiers and the disciples. One family member should represent the crowd that came for Jesus. One should be Peter. One should be Jesus. Take turns in each role, and have fun imagining what the scene was like.

ACTIVITY #2: SERVE AN ENEMY

Even though Jesus knew his enemies, he still stooped to love and to serve them. In what way can you serve or do something kind this week for someone who you might consider an enemy?

"I Am he."

The crowd that came for Jesus was astounded at his declaration, "I AM he."[4] Why? When Jesus answered, "I AM he," the crowd probably remembered a moment in the Old Testament when God revealed himself to Moses. Exodus 3:13–14 (NLT) says, "But Moses protested, 'If I go to the people of Israel and tell them, "The God of your ancestors has sent me to you," they will ask me, "What is his name?" Then what should I tell them?' God replied to Moses, 'I AM WHO I AM. Say this to the people of Israel: I AM has sent me to you.'" When Jesus answered, "I AM he," he claimed to be God himself, which for that crowd meant blasphemy. It was as good of a confession as the crowd could have hoped for.

I Don't Even Know the Man!

SETTING UP THE STORY

We've been reading stories of Jesus and Peter's relationship in the Gospels to see what we can learn about being a true friend. Jesus was honest with Peter. He encouraged Peter. He was willing to confront Peter when he did something wrong. He showed his true self to Peter. Even when his closest disciples floundered and stumbled, Jesus never gave up hope for them. He never stopped believing in them . . . even when they stopped believing in him. Today's story is the last time we meet Peter before Jesus's death and resurrection.

READ: LUKE 22:54–62 (MSG)

Arresting Jesus, they marched him off and took him into the house of the Chief Priest. Peter followed, but at a safe distance. In the middle of the courtyard some people had started a fire and were sitting around it, trying to keep warm. One of the serving maids sitting at the fire noticed him, then took a second look and said, "This man was with him!"

He denied it, "Woman, I don't even know him."

A short time later, someone else noticed him and said, "You're one of them."

But Peter denied it: "Man, I am not."

About an hour later, someone else spoke up, really adamant: "He's got to have been with him! He's got 'Galilean' written all over him."

Peter said, "Man, I don't know what you're talking about." At that very moment, the last word hardly off his lips, a rooster crowed. Just then, the Master turned and looked at Peter. Peter remembered what the Master had said to him: "Before the rooster crows, you will deny me three times." He went out and cried and cried and cried.

TALK ABOUT IT

- Why do you think Peter kept denying that he knew Jesus?
- How do you think Peter was feeling after Jesus was arrested?
- How do you think Peter felt after the rooster crowed?
- Have you ever let someone down? What did that feel like?
- If someone you loved denied knowing you, how would it make you feel?
- Is there anything that confuses you about this story? If so, it's okay! Let's talk about it.
- Do you have any questions about Luke 22:54–62?

CLOSING THOUGHT

Fear is a powerful emotion. After Jesus was arrested and taken away, Peter must have felt desperately afraid for Jesus. Peter was also desperately afraid for himself. Fear drove Peter to deny Jesus three times in order to spare his own life.

On the night of his arrest, Jesus told his disciples, "Peace I leave with you; my peace I give you. I do not give to you as the world gives. Do not let your hearts be troubled and do not be afraid" (John 14:27 NIV). Jesus knew that without God's love and peace, his disciples would be troubled and afraid. Jesus's trust in God made him able to stand firm in who he was in the face of trouble, while Peter was crippled by his own fear.

Peter might have felt like he could never be forgiven for abandoning Jesus. It will take Jesus's death and resurrection to strengthen Peter's faith. Jesus will restore Peter, and that love will empower Peter to love and live boldly. With Jesus, nothing is impossible!

PRAYER PROMPT

Jesus does not give up on Peter, even when he denied him three times. God's love is more powerful than our fear. When trouble comes, we can pray for the Holy Spirit to comfort and embolden us to stand firm in God's love and truth. Let's ask God to be with us when we are afraid and to help us love and forgive each other, even when we let each other down.

ACTIVITY #1: REPAIR BROKEN RELATIONSHIPS

If you've gotten into a fight with a friend or family member, maybe it's time to try to repair that friendship. It can be hard to set aside wanting to be the winner in a fight, but God calls us to humble ourselves, even when we believe we are right. Tell your friend what you think and how what happened made you feel, and then ask for forgiveness (or forgive that person).[5] It takes courage to make peace. You can do it!

ACTIVITY #2: MAKE A SCENE

Choose your favorite art materials to illustrate this scene—paint, markers, colored pencils, crayons, clay, Play-Doh—whatever you have handy. What images stand out to you in this story?

The Rule of Threes

Jesus prayed in the garden three times. The rooster crowed three times. Peter denied Jesus three times. For Jews, to do anything three times meant it was now permanent. Three is also the number of truth and balance—together God the Father, God the Son, and God the Holy Spirit connect in the Trinity (or three in one). Three can also symbolize harmony and reconciliation.[6] The next time Peter and Jesus talked in the Gospels, it was after Jesus's resurrection. Jesus asked Peter three times if he loved him, and three times he answered yes. The next time you see the number three in the Bible, think about what it might mean.

Section 4

IN THE FAMILY

John the Baptist versus Jesus the Baptist

SETTING UP THE STORY

There's a lot to learn about relationships with family members from how Jesus interacted with family. We'll begin with John the Baptist. Jesus's mother, Mary, was a relative of John's mom, Elizabeth. Jesus and John the Baptist have a lot in common: angels greeted both of their parents before they were born to announce their special calling, they were likely raised together in the same extended family, they were close in age, and they were both in ministry. Let's find out what John the Baptist had to say about his relative, Jesus.

READ: JOHN 3:22–36 (NIV)

After this, Jesus and his disciples went out into the Judean countryside, where he spent some time with them, and baptized. Now John also was baptizing at Aenon near Salim, because there was plenty of water, and people were coming and being baptized. (This was before John was put in prison.) An argument developed between some of John's disciples and a certain Jew over the matter of ceremonial washing. They came to John and said to him, "Rabbi, that man who was with you on the other side of the Jordan—the one you testified about—look, he is baptizing, and everyone is going to him."

To this John replied, "A person can receive only what is given them from heaven. You yourselves can testify that I said, 'I am not the Messiah but am sent ahead of him.' The bride belongs to the bridegroom. The friend who attends the bridegroom waits and listens for him, and is full of joy when he hears the bridegroom's voice. That joy is mine, and it is now complete. He must become greater; I must become less."

The one who comes from above is above all; the one who is from the earth belongs to the earth, and speaks as one from the earth. The one who comes from heaven is above all. He testifies to what he has seen and heard, but no one accepts his testimony. Whoever has accepted it has certified that God is truthful. For the one whom God has sent speaks the words of God, for God gives the Spirit without limit. The Father loves the Son and has placed everything in his hands. Whoever believes in the Son has eternal life, but whoever rejects the Son will not see life, for God's wrath remains on them.

TALK ABOUT IT

- How might you feel if a bunch of your friends suddenly started spending time with someone else?
- Can you relate to the way the disciples reacted to Jesus baptizing people, just like John?
- What was John's response to his disciples when they told him about Jesus baptizing people on the other side of the river?
- What do you think John meant when he described himself as the one who attends the bridegroom?
- Have you ever done something that put the spotlight on someone else? How did that make you feel?
- Is there anything that confuses you about this story? If so, it's okay! Let's talk about it.
- Do you have any questions about John 3:22–36?

CLOSING THOUGHT

Before Jesus began teaching publicly, John the Baptist started his ministry out in the wilderness. He called people to turn back to God so that they were ready for Jesus's arrival. John was very popular; he was the star of the show out in the desert, and people flocked to him to be baptized.

But then Jesus started his ministry and began baptizing people too.

In the world's view of things, John should have felt threatened by Jesus's rise to fame. John's disciples expected that when they asked him what he thought about this new guy on the scene. It was his younger relative, after all, just some kid he grew up with, and now he was barging in on John's business.

But John the Baptist knew his true calling, which was to bring glory to Jesus. That's what he meant when he said, "He must become greater; I must become less." He wasn't threatened by Jesus at all. Instead, John used his position of power and influence to point people to the true Savior, Jesus, who is above all and speaks the words of God.

PRAYER PROMPT

God, sometimes it is hard for us not to envy others when the spotlight is on them. Help us to celebrate other people's successes, and give us opportunities to lift up others. Thank you for giving us the example of John the Baptist, who sought out glory for you and not praise for himself.

ACTIVITY #1: USE YOUR GIFTS

What is something you are really good at? Think of a way to use your gift to show God's love to others.

ACTIVITY #2: WORDS OF AFFIRMATION

Look for an opportunity to celebrate someone else this week. Tell that person why you appreciate them, and share that same thought with someone else you both know.

The Bride and the Bridegroom

The relationship between Jesus and God's people was sometimes described as a marriage. God's people are called the "bride of Christ," and Jesus called himself the "bridegroom." During Jesus's time, most marriages were arranged, meaning that the parents decided who would marry their son or daughter. Marriage was less about romantic love and more about survival, ensuring that your family would carry on to the next generation.

Weddings themselves usually lasted five to seven days! At the beginning of the celebration, the groom would gather his friends and go to his bride's father's house to fetch her for the wedding. In today's story, John the Baptist referred to himself as the best man, the one who attends the bridegroom. The best man coordinated the parade from the father's house to the festivities and stayed by the groom's side all throughout the celebration.

Reassuring Words for an Inmate

SETTING UP THE STORY

John the Baptist eventually found himself in trouble with the law in Judea. The ruler of Judea, Herod, had divorced his own wife and unlawfully married his brother's wife. John the Baptist openly disapproved of what Herod did. Herod wasn't about to put up with someone questioning his life choices, so he had John thrown in prison. John was not feeling great about how things were going for him. That's where we meet John and Jesus in today's story.

READ: MATTHEW 11:2–19 (NLT)

John the Baptist, who was in prison, heard about all the things the Messiah was doing. So he sent his disciples to ask Jesus, "Are you the Messiah we've been expecting, or should we keep looking for someone else?"

Jesus told them, "Go back to John and tell him what you have heard and seen—the blind see, the lame walk, those with leprosy are cured, the deaf hear, the dead are raised to life, and the Good News is being preached to the poor." And he added, "God blesses those who do not fall away because of me."

As John's disciples were leaving, Jesus began talking about him to the crowds. "What kind of man did you go into the wilderness to see? Was he a weak reed, swayed by every breath of wind? Or were you expecting to see a man dressed in expensive clothes? No, people with expensive clothes live in palaces. Were you looking for a prophet? Yes, and he is more than a prophet. John is the man to whom the Scriptures refer when they say,

'Look, I am sending my messenger ahead of you,
and he will prepare your way before you.'

"I tell you the truth, of all who have ever lived, none is greater than John the Baptist. Yet even the least person in the Kingdom of Heaven is greater than he is! And from the time John the Baptist began preaching until now, the Kingdom of Heaven has been forcefully advancing, and violent people are attacking it. For before John came, all the prophets and the law of Moses looked forward to this present time. And if you are willing to accept what I say, he is Elijah, the one the prophets said would come. Anyone with ears to hear should listen and understand!

"To what can I compare this generation? It is like children playing a game in the public square. They complain to their friends,

>   'We played wedding songs,
>   and you didn't dance,
>   so we played funeral songs,
>   and you didn't mourn.'

"For John didn't spend his time eating and drinking, and you say, 'He's possessed by a demon.' The Son of Man, on the other hand, feasts and drinks, and you say, 'He's a glutton and a drunkard, and a friend of tax collectors and other sinners!' But wisdom is shown to be right by its results."

TALK ABOUT IT

- When your life gets tough, how does it make you feel?
- How does Jesus encourage John the Baptist?
- What do you think Jesus meant when he said that the kingdom of heaven has been forcefully advancing until now?
- When Jesus describes John the Baptist, who does he say John is like?
- Do you ever feel like no matter what you do, some people will never accept you? How does that feel?
- Is there anything that confuses you about this story? If so, it's okay! Let's talk about it.
- Do you have any questions about Matthew 11:2–19?

CLOSING THOUGHT

In the last story, John the Baptist reassured his friends that Jesus was the real deal. Today it's Jesus who praised John the Baptist. With all of the bad things happening in John's life, he may have begun to have doubts about Jesus and the message. You can hear it in his question, "Are you the Messiah we've been expecting, or should we keep looking for someone else?"

Jesus sent a reassuring message and then turned to the crowd who, at this point, had just begun to witness his miracles. Jesus told the crowd that everything that had happened in history was leading to this moment: The Messiah is here! In the Old Testament, God promised that Elijah would announce the coming of the Lord (Malachi 4:5–6). Jesus called John the Baptist "Elijah" because he announced Jesus's coming! This was what they had been waiting centuries for, and yet nothing John the Baptist or Jesus did was good enough for the crowd. The people found fault in whatever way the two of them behaved. Jesus spoke up on behalf of his relative John and stood for the truth, even if it was hard.

PRAYER PROMPT

Praise God that he is a God of justice and mercy. Let's thank him for the example of Jesus defending the defenseless, standing up for the truth. Ask God for the courage to speak up when we see someone being treated wrongly. Ask for help seeing beyond the ways people act to who they are on the inside and loving them the way God loves them.

ACTIVITY #1: ENCOURAGE A PRISONER

If you know someone who is in prison right now, write them a letter to lift their spirits. If you don't know anyone in prison, you can find people who would like letters through Christian Pen Pals (www.Christian-Penpals .com), Evangel Prison Ministries (www.evangelprisonministries.org), or the ARM Program through Forgotten Man Ministries (www.forgottenman .org/authenticremoteministry), or reach out to your local law enforcement to ask how you can support local prisoners. Work as a family to come up with things you can safely share with prisoners: Bible verses, words of encouragement about God, and prayers for them are all good places to begin.

ACTIVITY #2: LEARN ABOUT JUSTICE AND MERCY

Like John, there are still people today who are sent to prison for crimes they didn't commit. With your parents' help, go online to The Innocence Project (www.innocenceproject.org) to learn about an organization that is trying to help people prove their innocence and be released from prison. Talk with your family about ways you can support organizations like this one.

John the Baptist's Old Testament Calling

Besides being Jesus's relative, John the Baptist had a reputation for being kind of a wild man! He wore clothes made from camel's hair and lived on locusts and wild honey. He called people to repent and be baptized as a public display of their commitment to follow God.

John's ministry fulfilled Old Testament prophecies about the coming Messiah. Matthew pointed to Isaiah's seven-hundred-year-old prophecy, "A voice of one calling: 'In the wilderness prepare the way for the Lord; make straight in the desert a highway for our God'" (Isaiah 40:3 NIV). Another prophet, Malachi, wrote, "'I will send my messenger, who will prepare the way before me. Then suddenly the Lord you are seeking will come to his temple; the messenger of the covenant, whom you desire, will come,' says the Lord Almighty" (Malachi 3:1 NIV).

Jesus after Hearing about John the Baptist

SETTING UP THE STORY

Jesus and John the Baptist had a special connection, as family members and as two men on a similar mission inviting people to follow God's ways. In today's story, something tragic happens to John the Baptist. The story in Matthew gives us a glimpse of what God's grief in the face of the world's injustice looks like. (Warning to parents: Today's Scripture might be difficult for younger children because it involves John's death. Proceed with caution.)

READ: MATTHEW 14:1–14 (NIV)

At that time Herod the Tetrarch heard the reports about Jesus, and he said to his attendants, "This is John the Baptist; he has risen from the dead! That is why miraculous powers are at work in him."

Now Herod had arrested John and bound him and put him in prison because of Herodias, his brother Philip's wife, for John had been saying to him: "It is not lawful for you to have her." Herod wanted to kill John, but he was afraid of the people, because they considered John a prophet.

On Herod's birthday the daughter of Herodias danced for the guests and pleased Herod so much that he promised with an oath to give her whatever she asked. Prompted by her mother, she said, "Give me here on a platter the head of John the Baptist." The king was distressed, but because of his oaths and his dinner guests, he ordered that her request be granted and had John beheaded in the prison. His head was brought in on a platter and given to the girl, who carried it to her mother. John's disciples came and took his body and buried it. Then they went and told Jesus.

When Jesus heard what had happened, he withdrew by boat privately to a solitary place. Hearing of this, the crowds followed him on foot from the towns. When Jesus landed and saw a large crowd, he had compassion on them and healed their sick.

TALK ABOUT IT

- Who did Herod think Jesus was at the beginning of today's story?
- How does Jesus handle the news about John's death?
- What does Jesus do when people start to show up where he retreated?
- When something bad happens, how does it make you feel?
- Is there anything that confuses you about this story? If so, it's okay! Let's talk about it.
- Do you have any questions about Matthew 14:1–14?

CLOSING THOUGHT

What happened to John the Baptist was wrong and terrible. Wrong and terrible things happen. It's very hard to understand why God lets bad things happen. His will is for all people to be free to make their own choices (even if those choices result in suffering), and his desire for us is to be in his presence. Even when terrible things happen, God is there, working to bring healing and restoration in ways we never could have imagined.

After Jesus heard the news about his relative, John, he went off to be alone. Sometimes we just need solitude to process what's happened, to cry, to ask God why, to be angry, and to feel all of the feelings.

Jesus's grief was interrupted by people trying to reach him. He could have ignored the needs of those who followed him and tended to his own pain. Instead, he had compassion for them. When terrible things happen, God does not abandon us. God is there to comfort us. Jesus turned his grief into compassion for those who were also hurting. Through the miraculous power of love and forgiveness, God can take our suffering and turn it into compassion.

PRAYER PROMPT

Lord, the world is filled with sorrow, but you came to bring light to the broken world. Thank you. Thank you for loving us so much and comforting us when we are sad, angry, and confused. Thank you for being by our side when things are hard and we can't understand what's happening. Help us to feel the same compassion you feel for the hurting world, so that we can bring encouragement, hope, and love to others.

ACTIVITY #1: IN MEMORY OF

Think of someone who has died and do something in their memory. Write a letter to someone they left behind letting them know you were thinking about them and remembering them, or give to a cause that mattered to them.

ACTIVITY #2: TELL A STORY

Parents, share with your child(ren) a time when something sad happened to you. How did you feel when it happened? How did that difficulty change you or shape you? What happened as a result of that event? Were you able to find God in the midst of the storm?

Herod the Tetrarch

Herod the Tetrarch was also known as Herod Antipas and King Herod (although he never actually held the title of king). He ruled over Galilee and Perea. Herod Antipas was also ruler over Galilee when Jesus was arrested and crucified.

Herod came from a family dominated by power and suspicion. People who seemed like a threat to their power were imprisoned or executed. One of his brothers had tried to poison their father. When Herod's father couldn't track down the newborn King Jesus, he had all of the infant sons in Bethlehem who were two years old or younger murdered. With that kind of a family, Herod Antipas was used to getting what he wanted and didn't let others stand in his way.

Even More Important than Family

SETTING UP THE STORY

Can you imagine what it would have been like to be the little brother or sister of Jesus, the Son of God? It must have been hard to hear an older brother claim to be the Savior of the world. In today's story, word had spread about Jesus. More and more people were seeking him out for help, and more and more people who were in charge of religious teaching at the time were coming to challenge Jesus. Let's see how Jesus's family reacted to all of this attention.

READ: MARK 3:20–35 (MSG)

Jesus came home and, as usual, a crowd gathered—so many making demands on him that there wasn't even time to eat. His friends heard what was going on and went to rescue him, by force if necessary. They suspected he was believing his own press.

The religion scholars from Jerusalem came down spreading rumors that he was working black magic, using devil tricks to impress them with spiritual power. Jesus confronted their slander with a story: "Does it make sense to send a devil to catch a devil, to use Satan to get rid of Satan? A constantly squabbling family disintegrates. If Satan were fighting Satan, there soon wouldn't be any Satan left. Do you think it's possible in broad daylight to enter the house of an awake, able-bodied man, and walk off with his possessions unless you tie him up first? Tie him up, though, and you can clean him out.

"Listen to this carefully. I'm warning you. There's nothing done or said that can't be forgiven. But if you persist in your slanders against God's Holy Spirit, you are repudiating the very One who forgives, sawing off the branch on which you're sitting, severing by your own perversity all connection with the One who forgives." He gave this warning because they were accusing him of being in league with Evil.

Just then his mother and brothers showed up. Standing outside, they relayed a message that they wanted a word with him. He was surrounded by the crowd when he was given the message, "Your mother and brothers and sisters are outside looking for you."

Jesus responded, "Who do you think are my mother and brothers?" Looking around, taking in everyone seated around him, he said, "Right here, right in front of you—my mother and my brothers. Obedience is thicker than blood. The person who obeys God's will is my brother and sister and mother."

TALK ABOUT IT

- Why do you think the religious scholars told people that Jesus was using "black magic"?
- How did Jesus respond to their accusations?
- What do you think it means to saw off the branch you're sitting on?
- How do you think Jesus's family members felt at the end of the story?
- Why do you think Jesus said what he did about family?
- Is there anything that confuses you about this story? If so, it's okay! Let's talk about it.
- Do you have any questions about Mark 3:20–35?

CLOSING THOUGHT

The things Jesus was saying to the religious leaders of the day were hard for them to hear. He challenged their authority. Jesus's family members were worried for his safety. They didn't want to see him get into trouble, but Jesus had his sights set on higher things than his personal well-being. Jesus was on a mission to show people God's love, and he wasn't going to let anyone or anything get in the way. Even though family is import-ant, Jesus told the crowd that obeying God's call to love is even more important.

Jesus had strong words for the religious leaders who were spreading lies about him, calling him evil. Whenever someone lies about a good person, we are naturally offended for them and want to come to their defense. How dare people spread rumors and call them something they aren't! That's why Jesus is so direct about the consequences of calling the work of the Holy Spirit "evil." Calling evil "good" and good "evil" creates all kinds of problems in the world. To say that the work of the Holy Spirit is bad is to call God himself bad, and that's serious!

PRAYER PROMPT

Let's ask God to open our eyes to the work of the Holy Spirit so that we can see God's goodness wherever it is, even when it doesn't look the way we expect it to. Let's pray that God would make us a family that lives to pursue his love and truth.

ACTIVITY #1: GOOD VERSUS EVIL

Draw a line down the center of a sheet of paper. Write down things that are good on one side and things that are evil on the other. Then flip the paper over and draw what you think it looks like for good to battle against evil.

ACTIVITY #2: TEAMWORK

It's easier to build something together than when you're working against each other, right? Find a puzzle, a model-car project, a Lego set, or some other building project and work together to finish it.

Religion Scholars from Jerusalem

The scholars who were spreading rumors and lies about Jesus came from Jerusalem, the center of Jewish leadership. The folks who lived in Capernaum—the city where Jesus lived as an adult—would have been in awe of these scholars. Think of the most powerful people in your country coming to visit your community today. We tend to pay attention and listen to people like that.

It took the scholars about four days to walk from Jerusalem to Capernaum.[1] They traveled all this way because they disagreed with Jesus's teaching and wanted to put a stop to his message. Even though they were spreading these rumors about Jesus in the community, Jesus still met with them. He reasoned with them and sought to explain how off-base their thinking was. Jesus would continue to disagree with the religious scholars all the way until his arrest and trial.

Coming Home to Nazareth

SETTING UP THE STORY

Just like today, there were plenty of people who didn't believe in Jesus, even when he walked and taught among them. We like to think that if we had met Jesus in person, we would have been among his followers, but even those who were related to him had a hard time believing. On top of that, when the religious scholars came from Jerusalem, they sowed even more seeds of doubt into the community. In today's story, Jesus returned to Nazareth to teach. Let's find out how the community received him.

READ: MARK 6:1–6 (NLT)

Jesus left that part of the country and returned with his disciples to Nazareth, his hometown. The next Sabbath he began teaching in the synagogue, and many who heard him were amazed. They asked, "Where did he get all this wisdom and the power to perform such miracles?" Then they scoffed, "He's just a carpenter, the son of Mary and the brother of James, Joseph, Judas, and Simon. And his sisters live right here among us." They were deeply offended and refused to believe in him.

Then Jesus told them, "A prophet is honored everywhere except in his own hometown and among his relatives and his own family." And because of their unbelief, he couldn't do any miracles among them except to place his hands on a few sick people and heal them. And he was amazed at their unbelief.

TALK ABOUT IT
- Why didn't the people in Jesus's hometown believe in him?
- Are you surprised that many of Jesus's family and neighbors didn't believe in him? Why?

- Have you ever felt like someone just didn't understand you? How did that feel?
- What do you think Jesus meant when he said, "A prophet is honored everywhere except in his own hometown"?
- Why couldn't Jesus perform miracles among them?
- Is there anything that confuses you about this story? If so, it's okay! Let's talk about it.
- Do you have any questions about Mark 6:1–6?

CLOSING THOUGHT

The people in Jesus's hometown of Nazareth struggled to believe that Jesus was who he said he was. They had known Jesus and his family since his birth! He was the son of Mary. They knew his brothers and sisters. Not too long ago, he was just a boy learning carpentry from his dad.

Family members can be our greatest source of support or the ones who doubt us most. It can be hard to believe that a person "just like us" can grow up to do amazing and miraculous things. Sometimes the source of that unbelief is envy, sometimes it's pride, and sometimes it's bitterness. These are all things that get in our way of loving other people and of other people receiving our love.

The miracles of Jesus were only limited by what people believed about him. The miracles of love today are only limited by what people believe as well. When we allow the Holy Spirit to help us get over our pride, bitterness, envy, and greed, love melts our hearts and makes a way for the miracles of Jesus.

PRAYER PROMPT

Let's ask God to help us to always support each other, and to forgive us for the times we've allowed pride or envy to tear each other down. May we build each other up and partner with God in miracle-making by loving people.

ACTIVITY #1: I'VE GOT YOUR BACK!

Share something that you want to do when you grow up (or, for parents, what you want to accomplish next). After you've shared, remind each other that you have each other's backs. Encourage each other to keep pursuing the dreams God has placed on your hearts.

ACTIVITY #2: LOVE SOMEONE

Even though people around Jesus refused to believe in him, that didn't stop Jesus from trying to perform miracles. Think of someone you have a hard time loving, and commit to being kind to that person this week. What is one thing you can do differently in the way you love that person?

James, the Brother of Jesus

Jesus's brother, James, struggled to believe in his big brother throughout Jesus's life. As the second oldest in the family, James (along with the rest of his family) was constantly worried about and questioning why Jesus was putting his life on the line for his beliefs. After Jesus rose from the dead, though, he appeared to James, which must have been quite the awakening! James grew into one of Jesus's most influential disciples. He led the church in Jerusalem along with Peter. He was a key decision maker in the early church, and the book of James in the New Testament is a letter that some say was written by him as well. James was martyred (or killed for his beliefs) in AD 62.[2]

All In for Jesus

SETTING UP THE STORY

Jesus's family had a complicated relationship with him when he was teaching out in the world. They were worried for his life and worried about his reputation. People thought he was a crazy person! Jesus bewildered his family members—they just didn't always know what to make of him. Your family is supposed to be a place of love, safety, and comfort, but in today's story, Jesus has some challenging things to say about family and loving God. Let's see what God has to teach us about how much he values us and how we are to put our relationship with him first in our lives.

READ: MATTHEW 10:30–42 (MSG)

"What's the price of a pet canary? Some loose change, right? And God cares what happens to it even more than you do. He pays even greater attention to you, down to the last detail—even numbering the hairs on your head! So don't be intimidated by all this bully talk. You're worth more than a million canaries.

"Stand up for me against world opinion and I'll stand up for you before my Father in heaven. If you turn tail and run, do you think I'll cover for you?

"Don't think I've come to make life cozy. I've come to cut—make a sharp knife-cut between son and father, daughter and mother, bride and mother-in-law—cut through these cozy domestic arrangements and free you for God. Well-meaning family members can be your worst enemies. If you prefer father or mother over me, you don't deserve me. If you prefer son or daughter over me, you don't deserve me.

"If you don't go all the way with me, through thick and thin, you don't deserve me. If your first concern is to look after yourself, you'll never find yourself. But if you forget about yourself and look to me, you'll find both yourself and me.

"We are intimately linked in this harvest work. Anyone who accepts what you do, accepts me, the One who sent you. Anyone who accepts what I do accepts my Father, who sent me. Accepting a messenger of God is as good as being God's messenger. Accepting someone's help is as good as giving someone help. This is a large work I've called you into, but don't be overwhelmed by it. It's best to start small. Give a cool cup of water to someone who is thirsty, for instance. The smallest act of giving or receiving makes you a true apprentice. You won't lose out on a thing."

TALK ABOUT IT

- How much does Jesus say that God cares for you?
- When Jesus said that he didn't come to "make life cozy," how does that make you feel?
- What do you think Jesus meant by "well-meaning family members can be your worst enemies"?
- How much commitment does Jesus expect of his followers?
- What does Jesus tell his followers to do to get started following him?
- Is there anything that confuses you about this story? If so, it's okay! Let's talk about it.
- Do you have any questions about Matthew 10:30–42?

CLOSING THOUGHT

Jesus means business in today's story, doesn't he? As important as family is, Jesus told his disciples that following God is even more important. Jesus shared how much you are worth to God—more than a million canaries! He taught that no matter what other people say or do, you should stand up for God's love . . . even if that means standing up for God's love with your family members.

Jesus calls us to be "all in" for God's love, to pledge allegiance to his way of living in this world over everything else. That's a high calling! If we stop looking out for ourselves all of the time and begin to follow Jesus instead, we will find the love of God, and Jesus will help us find our true selves too.

All of us are connected in the work of sharing God's love, so we should not hesitate to accept help from others and to help each other out. But it doesn't have to be huge, dramatic acts of love—all it takes is one person doing small acts of kindness to spread God's love. If we commit to starting small, we can be messengers of God's love every single day.

PRAYER PROMPT

Let's thank God for how much he knows about us and cares about us. Ask the Holy Spirit to help us put the love of God before everything else, even before family. If there is a difficult relationship in your family, pray for help forgiving and loving that person, even if things are hard between you. Ask God to show us ways to put God's love into action in our daily lives.

ACTIVITY #1: A COOL CUP OF WATER

Jesus encouraged his followers to begin by offering a cool cup of water to someone who is thirsty. Contact a local food pantry or homeless shelter to find out about their needs. You might also look on the internet for organizations that strive to bring clean water to communities around the world. Some of these include Water Mission, Lifewater International, and Living Water International. Talk as a family about how you can support these ministries.

ACTIVITY #2: SPEAKING UP FOR GOD

Parents, share about a time in your life when you disagreed with someone about God. What was that like? Was it hard to speak up? What were the consequences of standing up for God? How did the other person receive your words?

The Worth of Little Birds

In other Bible translations, the word *canary* in today's story is sometimes translated "sparrow." The word is often used to refer to any common small bird that would have flown about in Jesus's time.[3] In biblical times and today, a sparrow is thought to be one of the smallest, most insignificant birds. They aren't very colorful, like other birds. They are common, kind of annoying, and cheap to buy. Sparrows are known to make messes with their nests in places people don't want them. In spite of how cheaply the world views the smallest of birds, God still takes care of them. If God cares for even these small birds, imagine how much more he cares for you, who is more valuable than a million canaries!

Who Gets to Be the Greatest?

SETTING UP THE STORY

Parents just want what is best for their kids. Sometimes what is best, though, isn't what they expected. In today's story, the mom of a couple of Jesus's disciples asked Jesus for a favor, but her idea of a great thing for her boys is very different from God's idea of greatness. Let's see what Jesus had to say to the mother of Zebedee's sons.

READ: MATTHEW 20:17–28 (NIV)

Now Jesus was going up to Jerusalem. On the way, he took the Twelve aside and said to them, "We are going up to Jerusalem, and the Son of Man will be delivered over to the chief priests and the teachers of the law. They will condemn him to death and will hand him over to the Gentiles to be mocked and flogged and crucified. On the third day he will be raised to life!"

Then the mother of Zebedee's sons came to Jesus with her sons and, kneeling down, asked a favor of him.

"What is it you want?" he asked.

She said, "Grant that one of these two sons of mine may sit at your right and the other at your left in your kingdom."

"You don't know what you are asking," Jesus said to them. "Can you drink the cup I am going to drink?"

"We can," they answered.

Jesus said to them, "You will indeed drink from my cup, but to sit at my right or left is not for me to grant. These places belong to those for whom they have been prepared by my Father."

When the ten heard about this, they were indignant with the two brothers. Jesus called them together and said, "You know that the rulers of the Gentiles lord it over them, and their high officials exercise authority over them. Not so with you. Instead, whoever wants to become great among you must be your servant, and whoever wants to be first must be your slave—just as the Son of Man did not come to be served, but to serve, and to give his life as a ransom for many."

TALK ABOUT IT

- What do you think the mom wanted for her sons?
- What do you think it means to drink from the same cup as Jesus?
- What are some things that define greatness in the world?
- How does Jesus define greatness?
- Is there anything that confuses you about this story? If so, it's okay! Let's talk about it.
- Do you have any questions about Matthew 20:17–28?

CLOSING THOUGHT

The mother in today's story truly wanted what was best for her sons. Jesus was leading a whole group of people who probably wanted the same thing. People who are following a leader want to have the same power and influence as that leader. They expect to walk in their footsteps or take over when the leader is gone.

Jesus told the mom that she didn't know what she was asking for. Leadership in God's kingdom looks really different from how the world defines leadership and success. The world defines greatness by how much power a person has, how much money they make, how they are able to influence others, or how famous they are.

To be great in God's kingdom, Jesus called people to be servants to others, which is the exact opposite of your typical leader. Serving others requires us to set aside our wishes for ourselves in order to put the wishes of others first. Jesus served people in the ultimate way: he laid down his life for his followers to demonstrate the greatness of God's love. Jesus calls us into that same level of sacrifice in order to be great in God's kingdom.

PRAYER PROMPT

Lord, help us to surrender our vision of what success looks like to you. Show us how we can be great according to your ways. Thank you for the example you've shown us in Jesus Christ, who showed us what it looks like to love and serve others.

ACTIVITY #1: NO, YOU GO FIRST

Think about the times you have tried to be the first: in line, for dinner, for treats, and so on. The next time you have an opportunity to be first, try to give someone else your spot.

ACTIVITY #2: SELFLESS SERVICE

Talk with your family about ways that you can serve each other in your home. Everyone, volunteer one way you can be a servant to your family this week and then practice this activity.

Salome, the Wife of Zebedee

The mother of James and John (Zebedee's sons) in today's story is also called Salome (pronounced sa-LOHM-ay) in other parts of the Gospels. She played an important role in Jesus's life, death, and resurrection. Besides being the mom of two of the disciples, she was also one of Jesus's followers who ministered to (or took care of) Jesus. She probably hosted the disciples in her home when they were in Galilee.

Along with Mary Magdalene and Mary the mother of Jesus, Salome was one of the many women who were at Jesus's side when he was being crucified. She was also called the sister of Mary, the mother of Jesus, which may have meant that she was Jesus's aunt! Salome was one of the women who went to the tomb to anoint Jesus's body after he was buried but discovered instead that the stone had been rolled away and his tomb was empty.[4]

Section 5

LOVING
OUR ENEMIES

Thirty Pieces of Silver

SETTING UP THE STORY

One of the hardest things Jesus taught about God's love is that we aren't only supposed to love our friends, family, neighbors, and other people we like, we're also supposed to love people who aren't easy to love. We're supposed to love people who are mean. We're supposed to love people who are out to get us. We're even supposed to love the people who want to hurt us. One of the people who turned against Jesus was one of his closest disciples. Let's see what we can learn about loving our enemies from the way Jesus interacted with Judas.

READ: MATTHEW 26:14–30 (NLT)

Then Judas Iscariot, one of the twelve disciples, went to the leading priests and asked, "How much will you pay me to betray Jesus to you?" And they gave him thirty pieces of silver. From that time on, Judas began looking for an opportunity to betray Jesus.

On the first day of the Festival of Unleavened Bread, the disciples came to Jesus and asked, "Where do you want us to prepare the Passover meal for you?"

"As you go into the city," he told them, "you will see a certain man. Tell him, 'The Teacher says: My time has come, and I will eat the Passover meal with my disciples at your house.'" So the disciples did as Jesus told them and prepared the Passover meal there.

When it was evening, Jesus sat down at the table with the Twelve. While they were eating, he said, "I tell you the truth, one of you will betray me."

Greatly distressed, each one asked in turn, "Am I the one, Lord?"

He replied, "One of you who has just eaten from this bowl with me will betray me. For the Son of Man must die, as the Scriptures declared long ago. But how terrible it will be for the one who betrays him. It would be far better for that man if he had never been born!"

Judas, the one who would betray him, also asked, "Rabbi, am I the one?" And Jesus told him, "You have said it."

As they were eating, Jesus took some bread and blessed it. Then he broke it in pieces and gave it to the disciples, saying, "Take this and eat it, for this is my body."

And he took a cup of wine and gave thanks to God for it. He gave it to them and said, "Each of you drink from it, for this is my blood, which confirms the covenant between God and his people. It is poured out as a sacrifice to forgive the sins of many. Mark my words—I will not drink wine again until the day I drink it new with you in my Father's Kingdom."

Then they sang a hymn and went out to the Mount of Olives.

TALK ABOUT IT

- How much did the priests pay Judas Iscariot to betray Jesus?
- How did Jesus respond when Judas asked him, "Rabbi, am I the one?"
- Why do you think Jesus let Judas be part of the twelve disciples if he knew that Judas would eventually betray him?
- Have you ever felt betrayed by a friend? How did it feel? (*Betray* means to put someone in danger by turning over information about them to an enemy.)
- What did Jesus say the cup of wine symbolized during the Last Supper?
- Is there anything that confuses you about this story? If so, it's okay! Let's talk about it.
- Do you have any questions about Matthew 26:14–30?

CLOSING THOUGHT

It's hard to imagine that Jesus could still sit around a table eating dinner, knowing there was a person with him—one of his closest followers—who was going to turn him over to be killed. And yet that's exactly what Jesus did. Jesus still led the Passover Feast. Jesus even shared with the disciples that the events about to happen after dinner needed to happen in order to fulfill Scripture. Jesus knew that his sacrifice was necessary for the unbelieving world to finally understand who God truly is and how much he truly loves them.

Even though Jesus's death and resurrection were known by God before the beginning of time, Judas had a choice in whether to be part of that betrayal. The priests could have arrested Jesus all on their own; they didn't need to conspire with Judas. Maybe that's why Jesus allowed Judas to remain in his close circle of friends; maybe Jesus hoped Judas would change his mind and make the right decision.

Even when Jesus knew that Judas would betray him, he still did not reject Judas. God never gives up hope on us either. No one is beyond God's great love.

PRAYER PROMPT

Let's thank God for never closing the door to his love and for giving us opportunities to turn back to him. Ask God for help from the Holy Spirit to show that same love to those who have hurt us. Pray for forgiveness for the wrong choices we've made that have hurt others, and ask God to help us remember his constant and never changing love for us.

ACTIVITY #1: BREAD AND WINE (OR GRAPE JUICE)

The meal that Jesus shared with his disciples is now celebrated by Christians everywhere as Communion (or Eucharist). Put together a mini-Communion meal with your family. Before you eat the bread, share one thing you love about God with your family. Before you drink the wine or grape juice, confess one thing you did that was wrong this week that has been bothering you. Remember that you don't have to carry it anymore. God forgives us for our sin and doesn't hold it against us.

ACTIVITY #2: TWO TRUTHS AND A LIE

Judas already knew his plans when he asked Jesus if he'd be the one to betray him. Play a game with your family where you tell each other two truths and one lie. See if you can guess which of the things about your family members are true and which is a lie.

The Festival of Unleavened Bread

The Jewish people have celebrated the Festival of Unleavened Bread, or Passover, for thousands of years. It is a weeklong celebration to remember God's faithfulness in rescuing his people from slavery in Egypt. The Jews needed to flee Egypt so quickly that there wasn't time for the bread dough to rise, which is why there is no yeast used during the festival week. The second major tradition of the festival is the sacrificial lamb. The Jews sacrificed a lamb to remember the blood over the doorway of their homes that protected the Jewish firstborns from one of the ten plagues. The lamb spared them their lives.

For Christians, Jesus became the sacrificial lamb of Passover. He gave himself for us so that our lives would be spared and we could experience the freedom from our slavery to sin.

A Friend's Betrayal

SETTING UP THE STORY

In the last story, Jesus called out Judas in front of everyone around the table. He pointed out that someone in the group would betray him and then continued with the Passover Feast. Today's story is from the book of John, another one of the Gospels. Let's read on to see how Jesus was affected by knowing that Judas would betray him and how Jesus treated Judas in spite of that information.

READ: JOHN 13:18–30 (MSG)

"I'm not including all of you in this. I know precisely whom I've selected, so as not to interfere with the fulfillment of this Scripture:

The one who ate bread at my table

Will stab me in the back.

"I'm telling you all this ahead of time so that when it happens you will believe that I am who I say I am. Make sure you get this right: Receiving someone I send is the same as receiving me, just as receiving me is the same as receiving the One who sent me."

After he said these things, Jesus became visibly upset, and then he told them why. "One of you is going to betray me."

The disciples looked around at one another, wondering who on earth he was talking about. One of the disciples, the one Jesus loved dearly, was reclining against him, his head on his shoulder. Peter motioned to him to ask who Jesus might be talking about. So, being the closest, he said, "Master, who?"

Jesus said, "The one to whom I give this crust of bread after I've dipped it." Then he dipped the crust and gave it to Judas, son of Simon the Iscariot. As soon as the bread was in his hand, Satan entered him.

"What you must do," said Jesus, "do. Do it and get it over with."

No one around the supper table knew why he said this to him. Some thought that since Judas was their treasurer, Jesus was telling him to buy what they needed for the Feast, or that he should give something to the poor.

Judas, with the piece of bread, left. It was night.

TALK ABOUT IT

- Who chose Judas to betray Jesus?
- Why did Jesus tell the disciples about the coming betrayal?
- How did Jesus feel about knowing Judas would betray him?
- What happened when Jesus gave Judas a piece of bread?
- Have you ever had someone reject your love? How did that feel?
- Is there anything that confuses you about this story? If so, it's okay! Let's talk about it.
- Do you have any questions about John 13:18–30?

CLOSING THOUGHT

Even though God loved Judas, God's heart still broke over that betrayal. The same is true for us when we try to love our enemies. Just because we love someone doesn't mean that their behavior doesn't hurt us. The reverse is true too—just because someone hurts us doesn't mean we can't love them. Even the Son of God was upset by betrayal. And even the Son of God still loved Judas.

No one can make a person love someone else . . . not even Jesus. It is a choice we each freely make. When Jesus offered Judas the piece of bread, it was an expression of love and friendship. Even up to this point, Judas could have made a different choice. In that moment, Judas rejected Jesus's love. In that moment, Jesus let Judas go. When you love someone and that love isn't returned, sometimes all you can do is release them from your expectations. Jesus knew what came next and what Judas was capable of, and still he gave him permission to leave.

With a hardened heart, Judas carried the piece of bread out of the room with him, uneaten.

PRAYER PROMPT

Let's thank God for his example in Jesus Christ, who despite knowing the contents of Judas's heart, loved him anyway. If there is someone who has rejected your love for them, ask God to comfort you and help you recover. Let's pray for God to soften our own hearts to the people in our life whom we have a hard time loving.

ACTIVITY #1: GUESS WHO

The disciples gathered with Jesus would never have guessed that Judas was the one who would betray Jesus. Play a guessing game with your family: Each person should write three things about themselves on a note card. Shuffle the note cards and then read off the three things to your family. Can you guess who each note card describes?

ACTIVITY #2: WHAT LOVE LOOKS LIKE

Love is not always easy. Look up 1 Corinthians 13:4–8. Which parts of this definition of love seem the hardest to do? Make a sign with these verses on them to hang up in your house.

"Satan Entered Him"

People have different opinions about what happened to Judas during the Passover meal. Some believe that the statement, "Satan entered him" means that Judas was literally possessed by the devil to complete the act of betrayal. The decisions Judas had made up to that point invited Satan to take possession of him and do Satan's bidding. Some believe that Judas was chosen by God explicitly for the purpose of fulfilling Scripture and therefore God allowed Judas to be possessed by Satan to complete the betrayal. Others think that it was at this moment Judas decided in his heart to go through with betraying Jesus, officially turning his back on his friend and leader. By turning away from God, Judas chose to follow the ways of darkness instead, so metaphorically speaking, Satan entered him. No matter what, Judas made a decision to betray Jesus, and it broke Jesus's heart.

Betrayed with a Kiss

SETTING UP THE STORY

Shortly after the Passover Feast, Jesus went out to the garden of Gethsemane to pray. Jesus told Peter, James, and John—the three disciples who came with him—to keep watch while he prayed, but they kept falling asleep! Jesus prayed three times for God to stop the coming events if it was his will, but since the beginning of time, the path to reveal God's true love to the world was already set. Today's story shows how Jesus responded to the crowd who came to arrest him. Let's see how Jesus loved his enemies in this moment.

READ: MATTHEW 26:47–56 (NIV)

While he was still speaking, Judas, one of the Twelve, arrived. With him was a large crowd armed with swords and clubs, sent from the chief priests and the elders of the people. Now the betrayer had arranged a signal with them: "The one I kiss is the man; arrest him." Going at once to Jesus, Judas said, "Greetings, Rabbi!" and kissed him.

Jesus replied, "Do what you came for, friend."

Then the men stepped forward, seized Jesus and arrested him. With that, one of Jesus' companions reached for his sword, drew it out and struck the servant of the high priest, cutting off his ear.

"Put your sword back in its place," Jesus said to him, "for all who draw the sword will die by the sword. Do you think I cannot call on my Father, and he will at once put at my disposal more than twelve legions of angels? But how then would the Scriptures be fulfilled that say it must happen in this way?"

In that hour Jesus said to the crowd, "Am I leading a rebellion, that you have come out with swords and clubs to capture me? Every day I sat in the temple courts teaching, and you did not arrest me. But this has all taken place that the writings of the prophets might be fulfilled." Then all the disciples deserted him and fled.

TALK ABOUT IT

- What did Judas do to signal which person was Jesus?
- What does Jesus call Judas when they greet each other?
- How does Jesus respond to his disciples when they try to come to his defense?
- Why do you think the crowd came with swords and clubs to capture Jesus?
- If you were one of Jesus's disciples, how do you think you would have reacted to his arrest?
- Is there anything that confuses you about this story? If so, it's okay! Let's talk about it.
- Do you have any questions about Matthew 26:47–56?

CLOSING THOUGHT

The crowd had seen Jesus teaching in the temple, and yet they came to arrest him under the cover of darkness. Can you imagine how the disciples and Jesus felt being approached by an angry mob carrying torches and clubs? It was probably a frightening and tense scene. The disciples knew Jesus hadn't committed a crime. When under threat, people either fight or flee. Peter, the disciple who drew his sword and cut off the ear of one of the servants, was ready to fight for Jesus. Peter was quick to defend Jesus and do what he thought was the right thing. But Jesus didn't want Peter to fight for him.

Jesus knew what needed to happen. He knew the crowd didn't understand who he was or what he came to do. He didn't get angry at the crowd. He didn't try to fight for his rights. He didn't even try to run away, like the disciples did at the end of the story. Jesus looked beyond the immediate trouble to the eternal promise of love and grace he knew mattered more than the suffering that was to come. There was no reason to fight—love is bigger even than death.

PRAYER PROMPT

Let's praise God for Jesus's love and compassion even when his own life was in danger. Let's ask God to help us surrender our fears and our anger when we're in trouble, to strive for peace and mercy even as we pray for justice to make things right.

ACTIVITY #1: LEGIONS OF ANGELS

Draw a picture of what you think a legion of angels would look like defending Jesus.

ACTIVITY #2: GUIDED BY LOVE

Everything Jesus did was guided by his love and faithfulness to God, even facing his enemies. Identify one person in your life you might describe as an enemy, or, if not an enemy, someone you often disagree with or who has hurt you. Commit to pray daily about that relationship, and ask God to help you figure out how to love that person.

Betrayed with a Kiss

Most of us greet friends and family with a hug or a handshake. In the first century, it was common for friends and companions to greet each other with a kiss on the cheek. It was a sign of brotherly love, honor, and respect. Judas was one of Jesus's closest friends. Under normal circumstances, Judas would have greeted Jesus with a kiss to honor him. In the garden of Gethsemane, though, Judas called Jesus "Rabbi" (or Teacher) and kissed him, not to honor him but to turn him over to the crowd who came to arrest Jesus.

Even at the moment of his betrayal, Jesus still looked on Judas with compassion and called him "friend." Isn't that love incredible?

Judas and the Chief Priests

SETTING UP THE STORY

As one of Jesus's closest disciples, Judas was one of Jesus's friends. At Passover, Jesus identified Judas as the one who would betray him, and Judas left the feast with a piece of uneaten bread in his hand. Then Judas betrayed Jesus with a kiss in the garden of Gethsemane and all of Jesus's followers fled the scene. Even after everything Judas did, Jesus never stopped loving him. The end of Judas's story is very sad. As Jesus was taken away, Judas was left to think about what just happened. (Warning, parents: Today's Scripture might be difficult for younger children because it involves Judas's death. Proceed with caution.)

READ: MATTHEW 27:1–10 (NLT)

Very early in the morning the leading priests and the elders of the people met again to lay plans for putting Jesus to death. Then they bound him, led him away, and took him to Pilate, the Roman governor.

When Judas, who had betrayed him, realized that Jesus had been condemned to die, he was filled with remorse. So he took the thirty pieces of silver back to the leading priests and the elders. "I have sinned," he declared, "for I have betrayed an innocent man."

"What do we care?" they retorted. "That's your problem."

Then Judas threw the silver coins down in the Temple and went out and hanged himself.

The leading priests picked up the coins. "It wouldn't be right to put this money in the Temple treasury," they said, "since it was payment for murder." After some discussion they finally decided to buy the potter's field, and they made it into a cemetery for foreigners. That is why the field is still called the Field of Blood. This fulfilled the prophecy of Jeremiah that says,

"They took the thirty pieces of silver—
the price at which he was valued by the people of Israel,
and purchased the potter's field,
as the LORD directed."

TALK ABOUT IT

- What does "remorse" mean?
- When Judas found out about Jesus's fate, what did he do?
- How did the leading priests react when Judas tried to return the silver?
- Have you ever done something wrong and tried to make up for it? How does it feel when someone rejects your effort to make amends?
- Parents, have you known someone who has died by suicide? If it's appropriate for the age of your child(ren), share with your family how that loss affected you.
- Is there anything that confuses you about this story? If so, it's okay! Let's talk about it.
- Do you have any questions about Matthew 27:1–10?

CLOSING THOUGHT

While Jesus awaited his sentence for committing no crime, Judas must have sat with the bag of coins in his lap and felt the weight of what had happened: he had turned over one of his closest friends to be killed. All of the ways Jesus had loved Judas probably ran through his mind.

When Judas returned the money and confessed that he betrayed an innocent man, he wanted to make things right. His confession should have cleared Jesus, but the chief priests didn't care. Judas couldn't bear the weight of knowing what he did, even after hearing for years the message of God's love. Judas's decision to end his life was tragic.

Judas is often villainized for his role in Jesus's arrest, but Jesus said over and over again that his death would fulfill Scripture. The battle throughout Jesus's life was not with Judas. Jesus came to show the world God's love, but the world wouldn't always hear it. The religious leaders were so committed to their way of understanding God that they couldn't see the Son of God right in front of them. We'll see that God's love extends even to these leaders.

PRAYER PROMPT

Let's thank God for hard stories that show us just how big his love is, that none of us are beyond his love and restoration. If you find it hard to receive God's love and forgiveness, pray that God would soften your heart and help you believe.

ACTIVITY #1: REMEMBER THE DEAD

Take a trip to a cemetery. If you live near a place where your family's loved ones are buried, visit their graves and reflect together on their lives. Bring flowers or other tokens of love to decorate their graves.

ACTIVITY #2: CONFESS AND FORGIVE

God's love is bigger than anything we could say or do, but sometimes, like Judas, it's hard for us to receive forgiveness. We can practice confession and forgiveness as a family. When a member of your family does something that hurts someone else (whether in word or action), take time to allow the offender to say what they did and to apologize to the offended (this is confession). When someone apologizes to you, acknowledge the hurt they caused and then release them from carrying the weight of their guilt by saying, "I forgive you," and letting go of the hurt. When we practice this together as a family in small ways, we learn how to receive God's love and forgiveness in all ways.

Fulfilling Scripture

There are many times when the Bible says that this happened to "fulfill Scripture." The Old Testament of the Bible has many stories that predicted the coming of a Savior. Prophecies were written in the Old Testament hundreds of years before Jesus was born as signs of things people should expect to happen when the Messiah arrived. For centuries, the Jews had been waiting for these things to come true. The gospel writers wanted their friends and neighbors to see how they actually had come true, in the life, death, and resurrection of Jesus, so that they would know the true God. The gospel of Matthew in particular is written for a Jewish audience and helps point readers to stories in the Old Testament that foretold Jesus's coming.

Forgive Them, Father

Before we read today's story, let's remember all of the ways Jesus loved people. He healed the broken and sick. He touched the untouchables. He cast out demons from possessed people. He talked to and taught women when the culture he lived in disregarded them. He raised people from the dead. He invited children to come to him when others thought they weren't worth his time. In his moment of betrayal, he continued to offer Judas friendship and love. This is our God, the God of love! Today we'll see how Jesus responds to people during the darkest moment of his life.

READ: LUKE 23:26–56 (MSG)

As they led him off, they made Simon, a man from Cyrene who happened to be coming in from the countryside, carry the cross behind Jesus. A huge crowd of people followed, along with women weeping and carrying on. At one point Jesus turned to the women and said, "Daughters of Jerusalem, don't cry for me. Cry for yourselves and for your children. The time is coming when they'll say, 'Lucky the women who never conceived! Lucky the wombs that never gave birth! Lucky the breasts that never gave milk!' Then they'll start calling to the mountains, 'Fall down on us!' calling to the hills, 'Cover us up!' If people do these things to a live, green tree, can you imagine what they'll do with deadwood?"

Two others, both criminals, were taken along with him for execution.

When they got to the place called Skull Hill, they crucified him, along with the criminals, one on his right, the other on his left.

Jesus prayed, "Father, forgive them; they don't know what they're doing."

Dividing up his clothes, they threw dice for them. The people stood there staring at Jesus, and the ringleaders made faces, taunting, "He saved others. Let's see him save himself! The Messiah of God—ha! The Chosen—ha!"

The soldiers also came up and poked fun at him, making a game of it. They toasted him with sour wine: "So you're King of the Jews! Save yourself!"

Printed over him was a sign: THIS IS THE KING OF THE JEWS.

One of the criminals hanging alongside cursed him: "Some Messiah you are! Save yourself! Save us!"

But the other one made him shut up: "Have you no fear of God? You're getting the same as him. We deserve this, but not him—he did nothing to deserve this."

Then he said, "Jesus, remember me when you enter your kingdom."

He said, "Don't worry, I will. Today you will join me in paradise."

By now it was noon. The whole earth became dark, the darkness lasting three hours—a total blackout. The Temple curtain split right down the middle. Jesus called loudly, "Father, I place my life in your hands!" Then he breathed his last.

When the captain there saw what happened, he honored God: "This man was innocent! A good man, and innocent!"

All who had come around as spectators to watch the show, when they saw what actually happened, were overcome with grief and headed home. Those who knew Jesus well, along with the women who had followed him from Galilee, stood at a respectful distance and kept vigil.

There was a man by the name of Joseph, a member of the Jewish High Council, a man of good heart and good character. He had not gone along with the plans and actions of the council. His hometown was the Jewish village of Arimathea. He lived in alert expectation of the kingdom of God. He went to Pilate and asked for the body of Jesus. Taking him down, he wrapped him in a linen shroud and placed him in a tomb chiseled into the rock, a tomb never yet used. It was the day before Sabbath, the Sabbath just about to begin.

The women who had been companions of Jesus from Galilee followed along. They saw the tomb where Jesus' body was placed. Then they went back to prepare burial spices and perfumes. They rested quietly on the Sabbath, as commanded.

TALK ABOUT IT

- Have you ever been mocked? How did that make you feel? How did you respond?
- How did Jesus respond to the people who crucified and mocked him?
- What did the second criminal ask Jesus to do?
- How did Jesus respond to the criminal?
- What was the reaction of the crowd after Jesus died?
- Is there anything that confuses you about this story? If so, it's okay! Let's talk about it.
- Do you have any questions about Luke 23:26–56?

CLOSING THOUGHT

How great is the love of God! Doesn't it make your heart weep to think of Jesus—an innocent man and the Son of God—mocked and tortured on the cross? Jesus didn't fight back or beg to be taken down. Instead, he focused on the needs of those around him, even while he was in agony. He urged the women not to weep. He prayed for his torturers. He encouraged the believing criminal and said he would join Jesus in paradise.

Many people were crucified in Roman times, but they were being punished for crimes they actually committed. Jesus wasn't just innocent. He wasn't just a good man. He was the Son of God, dying on a cross. But that's not the end of the story! If it were, we would never have even heard the name of Jesus.

In an unexpected encore, Jesus conquered death and rose again, proving to all who doubted him that he was indeed the Son of God.

Whatever comes from the Son also comes from the Father. God calls us to a life dedicated to following Jesus and loving others the way he loved us. Sometimes that love seems impossible, but with God, all things are possible!

PRAYER PROMPT

Lord, what you endured on the cross is overwhelming to us. We can hardly imagine it. Despite the physical and emotional pain, you showed the enormity of your compassion for this world by still looking out for the needs of the people around you, even your enemies. Teach us how to love the way you have loved us. By your Holy Spirit, fill our hearts with the same love for the world, even our enemies.

ACTIVITY #1: ILLUSTRATE THE SCENE

Artists throughout the centuries have painted the moment of Jesus's crucifixion. What do you think Skull Hill looked like? Draw or paint your perspective on the crucifixion of Jesus.

ACTIVITY #2: STEP INTO THE PAST

Choose one of the characters in the story today and tell the story from their point of view. You can write the story or share with your family what you think they were experiencing: What did they see and hear? What were they thinking? How did they feel before Jesus died, and how did they feel after?

The Temple Curtain

In the temple, a curtain separated people from the holy of holies, God's dwelling place on earth. The curtain was around sixty feet high, layered with blue, scarlet, and purple linen.[1]

The curtain symbolized the separation between people and God caused by sin. No one could go behind the curtain, except for one priest, just once a year. That priest crossed into the holy of holies to make atonement for (or repair the wrongs of) the sins of Israel.

Jesus's sacrifice on the cross was the final sacrifice—God repairing the wrongs for all humankind. That sacrifice tore the curtain in two and removed the separation between us and God, forever! No more would people need to make atonement for their wrongs, because Jesus threw out the scale, replacing it with grace and forgiveness.

Section 6

THE DISCIPLES AND THE RESURRECTED LORD

The Women at the Tomb

SETTING UP THE STORY

If the story of Jesus loving people had ended with the cross, he would have been just another really good person, known for his revolutionary love and acts of kindness, who was murdered by power-hungry rulers. But God's love is even bigger than death! He was buried in a tomb by Joseph of Arimathea and Nicodemus, two highly regarded Jews and members of the religious elite. Jesus could have revealed himself to these men after his resurrection; instead, he chose to show himself alive and raised from the dead to the unlikeliest disciples first.

READ: LUKE 24:1–12 (NIV)

On the first day of the week, very early in the morning, the women took the spices they had prepared and went to the tomb. They found the stone rolled away from the tomb, but when they entered, they did not find the body of the Lord Jesus. While they were wondering about this, suddenly two men in clothes that gleamed like lightning stood beside them. In their fright the women bowed down with their faces to the ground, but the men said to them, "Why do you look for the living among the dead? He is not here; he has risen! Remember how he told you, while he was still with you in Galilee: 'The Son of Man must be delivered over to the hands of sinners, be crucified and on the third day be raised again.'" Then they remembered his words.

When they came back from the tomb, they told all these things to the Eleven and to all the others. It was Mary Magdalene, Joanna, Mary the mother of James, and the others with them who told this to the apostles. But they did not believe the women, because their words seemed to them like nonsense. Peter, however, got up and ran to the tomb. Bending over, he saw the strips of linen lying by themselves, and he went away, wondering to himself what had happened.

TALK ABOUT IT

- If you visited the grave of a loved one and saw the headstone removed and the ground disturbed underneath, how would you react?
- What did the angels tell the women that helped them understand the empty tomb?
- What did Peter find when he entered the tomb?
- Why do you think the angels appeared to the women but not to the other disciples?
- Is there anything that confuses you about this story? If so, it's okay! Let's talk about it.
- Do you have any questions about Luke 24:1–12?

CLOSING THOUGHT

The women uncovered the most unlikely scene in the whole world when they arrived to find the tomb empty on Sunday morning after Jesus's death. They came to tend to Jesus's body and found the body missing! When they went to tell the other disciples what they had seen and heard from the angels, the disciples couldn't believe it.

Peter, the disciple who had just denied knowing Jesus three times in order to save his own skin, went to check it out for himself. All of the women who came to the tomb that Sunday morning had witnessed Jesus's death on the cross. They knew their dear friend and the Son of God should have been dead. The only logical answer to his missing body was that it had been stolen from the tomb.

But God's love defies logic. God's love left the tomb and greeted Mary Magdalene, the woman disciple who had been saved by Jesus long before he hung on the cross. God's love revealed itself to the faithful women who had walked with Jesus all the way to his death and beyond. The ones the world viewed as last got to hear the good news of his resurrection first.

PRAYER PROMPT

Let's thank God for the most surprising turn of events in all of history: the Son of God coming to earth, showing us the way of God's love, suffering on a cross for going against the religious order's view of God, and conquering death to be raised to life again. It's the most wonderful story ever, and it's the pathway for us to know God's love ourselves!

ACTIVITY #1: SURPRISE!

The angels delivered good news where the women expected bad. Think of a friend, neighbor, church member, or relative who could use a little pick-me-up, and deliver an unexpected letter, note, card, or gift to them to show you care.

ACTIVITY #2: BAKE RESURRECTION ROLLS

Buy a can of crescent roll dough and regular sized marshmallows. Wrap the crescent roll dough around a marshmallow, cover with cinnamon sugar, and bake as directed on the package. When the rolls are done, they'll be just as empty as the tomb Jesus left! Share your resurrection rolls with a friend as a special treat, telling them the story of Jesus's resurrection.

Mary Magdalene

Long before Jesus's death, he drove out seven demons from Mary Magdalene, a Jewish woman. After that, she was one of Jesus's most devoted followers. She is named over a dozen times in all four gospels, more than most of the other disciples. She was among the women who witnessed Jesus's death on the cross, and in John's story about the resurrection, Mary was the first person to see Jesus after he rose from the grave. In her grief, she didn't recognize Jesus at first and thought he was a gardener!

Walking on the Road
to Emmaus

SETTING UP THE STORY

The women began spreading the word about Jesus's resurrection immediately after they heard from the angels, but the eleven disciples thought
their testimony was crazy talk. When Jesus appeared to Mary Magdalene
outside of the tomb, she didn't recognize him. In today's story, two more of
Jesus's disciples don't immediately recognize him either. Let's see what the
risen Lord had to say to the two disciples on the road.

READ: LUKE 24:13–35 (MSG)

That same day two of them were walking to the village Emmaus, about
seven miles out of Jerusalem. They were deep in conversation, going over
all these things that had happened. In the middle of their talk and questions, Jesus came up and walked along with them. But they were not able
to recognize who he was.

He asked, "What's this you're discussing so intently as you walk along?"

They just stood there, long-faced, like they had lost their best friend.
Then one of them, his name was Cleopas, said, "Are you the only one in
Jerusalem who hasn't heard what's happened during the last few days?"

He said, "What has happened?"

They said, "The things that happened to Jesus the Nazarene. He was a
man of God, a prophet, dynamic in work and word, blessed by both God
and all the people. Then our high priests and leaders betrayed him, got him
sentenced to death, and crucified him. And we had our hopes up that he
was the One, the One about to deliver Israel. And it is now the third day
since it happened. But now some of our women have completely confused
us. Early this morning they were at the tomb and couldn't find his body.

They came back with the story that they had seen a vision of angels who said he was alive. Some of our friends went off to the tomb to check and found it empty just as the women said, but they didn't see Jesus."

Then he said to them, "So thick-headed! So slow-hearted! Why can't you simply believe all that the prophets said? Don't you see that these things had to happen, that the Messiah had to suffer and only then enter into his glory?" Then he started at the beginning, with the Books of Moses, and went on through all the Prophets, pointing out everything in the Scriptures that referred to him.

They came to the edge of the village where they were headed. He acted as if he were going on but they pressed him: "Stay and have supper with us. It's nearly evening; the day is done." So he went in with them. And here is what happened: He sat down at the table with them. Taking the bread, he blessed and broke and gave it to them. At that moment, open-eyed, wide-eyed, they recognized him. And then he disappeared.

Back and forth they talked. "Didn't we feel on fire as he conversed with us on the road, as he opened up the Scriptures for us?"

They didn't waste a minute. They were up and on their way back to Jerusalem. They found the Eleven and their friends gathered together, talking away: "It's really happened! The Master has been raised up—Simon saw him!"

Then the two went over everything that happened on the road and how they recognized him when he broke the bread.

TALK ABOUT IT

- Why do you think Jesus kept his real identity hidden from the two travelers on the road?
- How did Cleopas explain what happened to Jesus (who obviously already knew the details of his own story)?
- How did Jesus respond to the story about himself?
- At what point did the disciples finally recognize Jesus?
- Why do you think the breaking of bread opened the disciples' eyes?

- Is there anything that confuses you about this story? If so, it's okay! Let's talk about it.
- Do you have any questions about Luke 24:13–35?

CLOSING THOUGHT

The disciples were afraid for their own lives after seeing what the chief priests had done to Jesus. They were all mourning the loss of their leader and friend, and they were also grieving the lost hope they had that Jesus would save the Jewish people. They thought with the death of Jesus, the mission of their Messiah was ended, but Jesus had news for them!

It seems as if the risen Jesus kept his true identity hidden from his followers at first so that they could come to their own conclusion about who he really was. Maybe he wanted all of the truths he taught them over three years to stand on their own first. Once they had a chance to process his teaching about the prophecies in Scripture, only then did Jesus make himself fully known and open their eyes to who was in their presence.

After Jesus revealed himself and then left them alone, they remembered how they had felt talking with him on the road: *didn't we feel on fire as he conversed with us?* The Holy Spirit was opening their hearts to the truth and creating a sacred moment with Jesus even as their minds were still processing. Our encounters with holiness sometimes feel that way too. The Holy Spirit often works in community, creating bonds between believers and turning our spiritual conversations into sacred spaces for God to do his work.

PRAYER PROMPT

Let's thank God for the way we're given the freedom to figure out the truth about him, and that he reveals himself to us at just the right time in our lives. Ask God to prepare our hearts and open our eyes to the presence of the Holy Spirit all around us.

ACTIVITY #1: I SPY

God shows his presence in all kinds of ways in the world. This week when you gather with your family for dinner, share one way you saw evidence of God's love during the day. Think about conversations you had or things you observed in nature, or something else entirely.

ACTIVITY #2: WALK TO EMMAUS

The disciples had one of the most important conversations of their lives while walking to Emmaus. Take a walk with your family around your neighborhood or in a park. Leave behind any electronics so that you can be fully present with your family.

Breaking Bread with Jesus

The last time that Jesus ate with the disciples was the Passover Feast. During the Last Supper, Jesus had told the disciples to remember him every time they ate bread or drank wine. From now on, the bread symbolized his body, broken for them, and the wine symbolized his blood, poured out for them for the forgiveness of sins. The disciples didn't recognize Jesus when he walked with them on the road. They didn't recognize him when he revealed to them all the places in Scripture that pointed to his death and resurrection. It wasn't until he broke bread with them around the table that they saw Jesus in front of them, their eyes and hearts opened by the memory of broken bread and poured-out wine.

Jesus Appears to the Disciples

SETTING UP THE STORY

Despite eyewitness reports from the women, the apostles couldn't believe the talk that Jesus was raised from the dead. The Lord had told them what to expect, but among all of the dinners and miracles, healings and parables, the disciples had either forgotten or couldn't believe that Jesus would die and then come back to life. Maybe it seemed like too much to hope for. After the women shared what they saw at the tomb and the disciples on the road to Emmaus told them about their encounter with Jesus, the disciples were greeted by a very special guest.

READ: LUKE 24:36–49 (NIV)

While they were still talking about this, Jesus himself stood among them and said to them, "Peace be with you."

They were startled and frightened, thinking they saw a ghost. He said to them, "Why are you troubled, and why do doubts rise in your minds? Look at my hands and my feet. It is I myself! Touch me and see; a ghost does not have flesh and bones, as you see I have."

When he had said this, he showed them his hands and feet. And while they still did not believe it because of joy and amazement, he asked them, "Do you have anything here to eat?" They gave him a piece of broiled fish, and he took it and ate it in their presence.

He said to them, "This is what I told you while I was still with you: Everything must be fulfilled that is written about me in the Law of Moses, the Prophets and the Psalms."

Then he opened their minds so they could understand the Scriptures. He told them, "This is what is written: The Messiah will suffer and rise from the dead on the third day, and repentance for the forgiveness of sins will be preached in his name to all nations, beginning at Jerusalem. You are witnesses of these things. I am going to send you what my Father has promised; but stay in the city until you have been clothed with power from on high."

TALK ABOUT IT

- What did the disciples think when they first saw Jesus among them?
- How do you think you would have reacted to Jesus appearing in the room?
- Why did Jesus ask to eat a piece of fish?
- If we're looking for evidence to understand more about everything that happened to Jesus, where does he tell us to look?
- What does Jesus promise is going to happen next?
- Is there anything that confuses you about this story? If so, it's okay! Let's talk about it.
- Do you have any questions about Luke 24:36–49?

CLOSING THOUGHT

When the unexpected happens, it takes some time to believe it. We need more evidence. Jesus could see this about the disciples. Some of them had watched Jesus die just three days earlier. They were deep in grief and shock, so much so that when Jesus appeared to them, they couldn't believe their own eyes!

Thankfully, God didn't leave the truth about Jesus up to our own experiences. When the disciples doubted their own senses, Jesus took a bite of fish to prove he wasn't a ghost. Then he opened up their minds to centuries of stories and verses that pointed toward Jesus as the true Son of God. Jesus combined everything the disciples had experienced over three years with the Scriptures that had always guided their lives to give them a new and stronger foundation for their faith. Then he promised them even more: the coming of the Holy Spirit to give them confidence and power to spread the good news about Jesus to the world.

He has given us all of these things as well: our day-to-day experiences, centuries of wisdom and faith stories, and the Holy Spirit to guide us. What a wonderful God we serve!

PRAYER PROMPT

Let's thank God for the stories about his people and Jesus that have been collected in the Bible to help us know God better. Let's also thank God for the ways he reveals himself to us through the Holy Spirit and the world around us. God provides us so many ways to learn about, see, and experience the love of Christ! Let's ask God to open our eyes to all of the wonders and mysteries in the universe today.

ACTIVITY #1: FISH DINNER

Prepare together a fish dinner and invite friends to join in for a fish fry!

ACTIVITY #2: WISDOM SEARCH

Jesus pointed the apostles back to their Scriptures to help support their understanding of who he is. Search through the books of Psalms and Proverbs. What nuggets of wisdom and knowledge stick out to you? Choose one to write down and post where you can be reminded of it and try to memorize it, so that it is always with you.

Seeing Ghosts

The disciples in today's story thought they saw a ghost. Other translations use the word *spirit*, from the Greek word *pneuma*.[1] This word appears many times throughout Scripture.

Jesus assured the disciples that he wasn't a ghost. Besides the Holy Spirit, most of the spirits that are talked about in the Bible are either angels or demons. The spiritual world is mysterious, with many unknowns, but we have a Holy Spirit who produces good fruit in us (Galatians 5:22–23) and promises to comfort and guide us, no matter what unknowns and mysteries we face.

The Scars Tell the Story

SETTING UP THE STORY

In his gospel, John also told the story of the night Jesus first appeared to the disciples. He remembered different details from the night, including some comments from Thomas, a disciple who wasn't there the first time Jesus appeared, and how Jesus proved to Thomas that it was really him.

READ: JOHN 20:19–29 (NLT)

That Sunday evening the disciples were meeting behind locked doors because they were afraid of the Jewish leaders. Suddenly, Jesus was standing there among them! "Peace be with you," he said. As he spoke, he showed them the wounds in his hands and his side. They were filled with joy when they saw the Lord! Again he said, "Peace be with you. As the Father has sent me, so I am sending you." Then he breathed on them and said, "Receive the Holy Spirit. If you forgive anyone's sins, they are forgiven. If you do not forgive them, they are not forgiven."

One of the twelve disciples, Thomas (nicknamed the Twin), was not with the others when Jesus came. They told him, "We have seen the Lord!"

But he replied, "I won't believe it unless I see the nail wounds in his hands, put my fingers into them, and place my hand into the wound in his side."

Eight days later the disciples were together again, and this time Thomas was with them. The doors were locked; but suddenly, as before, Jesus was standing among them. "Peace be with you," he said. Then he said to Thomas, "Put your finger here, and look at my hands. Put your hand into the wound in my side. Don't be faithless any longer. Believe!"

"My Lord and my God!" Thomas exclaimed.

Then Jesus told him, "You believe because you have seen me. Blessed are those who believe without seeing me."

TALK ABOUT IT

- Why were the disciples afraid of the Jewish leaders?
- What did Jesus give to the disciples?
- What do you think Jesus meant by "As the Father has sent me, so I am sending you"?
- How do you think you would react if all of your friends had seen Jesus but you missed it?
- How does Jesus prove to Thomas that it's really him?
- Is there anything that confuses you about this story? If so, it's okay! Let's talk about it.
- Do you have any questions about John 20:19–29?

CLOSING THOUGHT

Jesus appeared to the apostles at their very lowest point, frightened for their lives and lost after the man they had followed for three years was murdered. Now that the Jewish leaders had gotten Jesus, the disciples were sure they were going to come for them next. The first thing the resurrected Lord said to them continued the message he had brought before he died: peace. Their hearts were troubled, so "Peace be with you."

Jesus gave the disciples the Holy Spirit and urged them to continue showing God's love to the world the way that he did: boldly and fearlessly teaching, healing, and loving others from the freedom of grace that was theirs through Jesus Christ.

That same Holy Spirit lives in each of us. It compels us to love God and others in the same supernatural way we've seen Jesus love people throughout the Gospels. We are the blessed ones who believe without seeing, learning and experiencing God's love miles and centuries removed from when Jesus walked the earth. What a great blessing it is!

PRAYER PROMPT

Let's thank God for the gift of the Holy Spirit and the generous way God revealed himself to us, through the disciples who walked alongside Jesus, through the writers who captured the stories of his miracles, and through the many, many followers of Christ who have carried the message of Jesus forward to where we are today. Praise God for the many who believed without seeing firsthand the risen Lord, whose faith helps us believe too. Let's ask for the help of the Holy Spirit to continue doing the work God has given us to do.

ACTIVITY #1: DINNER PARTY WITH FELLOW FOLLOWERS OF CHRIST

The disciples gathered together to support one another after the terrible loss of Jesus. Little did they know that their grieving was about to turn to joy! Invite other followers of Jesus over for a dinner party to celebrate the joy of Christ's salvation.

ACTIVITY #2: STORIES IN SCARS

Jesus proved that it was really him by showing the disciples his scars. We all carry scars that remind us of hard things we've gone through. Share the story of one of your scars with your family. How did the injury happen and what did it feel like? Did anyone help you? How did it heal?

Doubting Thomas

Thomas often gets a bad rap as "Doubting Thomas," but actually, Thomas only wanted what the other disciples had already received: a firsthand, eyewitness experience of the risen Lord. All of the other disciples saw Jesus in the flesh; Thomas didn't want to miss out on that. Jesus graciously answered Thomas by revealing himself once more a week later. Thomas's declaration, "My Lord and my God!" is one of the most direct affirmations of Jesus's divinity in the Bible. Jesus doesn't scold Thomas for his unbelief but instead blesses all who come after Thomas who will rely on these and other stories to trust in the Lord our God.

Fishing and Feeding Sheep

SETTING UP THE STORY

Peter didn't end things well with Jesus before he died. Having denied knowing Jesus three times before he was crucified, Peter must have felt humbled and guilty. He was Jesus's most dedicated and passionate follower; how could he turn his back on Jesus? Jesus knows our hearts. God knows what we need to restore our relationship with him. Today we will read one of Jesus's final recorded appearances. He has just the right message to help Peter return to the path of walking with God.

READ: JOHN 21:1–19 (MSG)

After this, Jesus appeared again to the disciples, this time at the Tiberias Sea (the Sea of Galilee). This is how he did it: Simon Peter, Thomas (nicknamed "Twin"), Nathanael from Cana in Galilee, the brothers Zebedee, and two other disciples were together. Simon Peter announced, "I'm going fishing."

The rest of them replied, "We're going with you." They went out and got in the boat. They caught nothing that night. When the sun came up, Jesus was standing on the beach, but they didn't recognize him.

Jesus spoke to them: "Good morning! Did you catch anything for breakfast?"

They answered, "No."

He said, "Throw the net off the right side of the boat and see what happens."

They did what he said. All of a sudden there were so many fish in it, they weren't strong enough to pull it in.

Then the disciple Jesus loved said to Peter, "It's the Master!"

When Simon Peter realized that it was the Master, he threw on some clothes, for he was stripped for work, and dove into the sea. The other disciples came in by boat for they weren't far from land, a hundred yards or so, pulling along the net full of fish. When they got out of the boat, they saw a fire laid, with fish and bread cooking on it.

Jesus said, "Bring some of the fish you've just caught." Simon Peter joined them and pulled the net to shore—153 big fish! And even with all those fish, the net didn't rip.

Jesus said, "Breakfast is ready." Not one of the disciples dared ask, "Who are you?" They knew it was the Master.

Jesus then took the bread and gave it to them. He did the same with the fish. This was now the third time Jesus had shown himself alive to the disciples since being raised from the dead.

After breakfast, Jesus said to Simon Peter, "Simon, son of John, do you love me more than these?"

"Yes, Master, you know I love you."

Jesus said, "Feed my lambs."

He then asked a second time, "Simon, son of John, do you love me?"

"Yes, Master, you know I love you."

Jesus said, "Shepherd my sheep."

Then he said it a third time: "Simon, son of John, do you love me?"

Peter was upset that he asked for the third time, "Do you love me?" so he answered, "Master, you know everything there is to know. You've got to know that I love you."

Jesus said, "Feed my sheep. I'm telling you the very truth now: When you were young you dressed yourself and went wherever you wished, but when you get old you'll have to stretch out your hands while someone else dresses you and takes you where you don't want to go." He said this to hint at the kind of death by which Peter would glorify God. And then he commanded, "Follow me."

TALK ABOUT IT

- What did most of the disciples do for a living before they met Jesus?
- What happened when Jesus told the disciples to cast their nets, even after they had spent all night fishing without catching anything?

- Do you remember what Jesus told the disciples when he first called them to follow him?
- Why do you think Jesus asked Peter the same question three times?
- What do you think Jesus meant when he told Peter to feed his sheep?
- Is there anything that confuses you about this story? If so, it's okay! Let's talk about it.
- Do you have any questions about John 21:1–19?

CLOSING THOUGHT

Many of the disciples were fishermen before they followed Jesus. When he first called them, Jesus told the disciples they would become "fishers of men." Three years later, Jesus was gone and their ministry seemed over. They returned to their old occupation as fishermen. After a bad night out on the sea with no catch, Jesus showed up and gave them the catch of a lifetime! Jesus reminded the men about their new jobs, to carry the message of God's love to the world.

God sees the needs of his people and meets them in unique and surprising ways. Sometimes God connects with us through our prayers, sometimes in our thoughts, and sometimes through other people. In today's story, Jesus knew what was going on inside Peter. He knew Peter felt terrible about turning his back on Jesus. He didn't get angry with Peter. Instead, he reminded Peter about his role as a disciple: It's time to teach people. It's time to care for the other followers. It's time to step up. If Peter felt unworthy of his calling, Jesus called him right back into serving God.

God doesn't give up on us.

PRAYER PROMPT

Let's thank God that he meets us right where we are, just like he met the fishermen disciples on the shore of the Sea of Galilee. Thank God for his patience with us and how kind and gentle he is when we've done something to hurt our relationship with him. Ask God for help loving people the same way he loves us.

ACTIVITY #1: GO FISH

The disciples caught all kinds of fish after Jesus told them to let down their nets. Play the card game Go Fish with your family.

ACTIVITY #2: NO, REALLY, GO FISH

If you're the outdoorsy type, take it up a notch and actually go fishing! Discuss with your family what it might have meant to the disciples to become fishers of men.

Love Versus Love

The Greek language that the Gospels were written in used different words for different types of love. The word *phileō* meant the kind of love between friends, affectionate love, or brotherly love.[2] This is the word Peter used when Jesus asked him if Peter loved him. But Jesus's question wasn't about brotherly love. Jesus asked Peter if he *agapē* loved him. *Agapē* love is unconditional.[3] Jesus asked Peter twice whether he *agapē* loved him, but Peter replied that he *phileō* loved Jesus. Maybe Peter couldn't bring himself to say he loved Jesus unconditionally after his denial of him, even as Jesus invited him into that love. Jesus changed his question the third time; he asked Peter if he *phileō* loved Jesus. God's love for us is *agapē* love. Through Christ, we can love others with that same *agapē* love.

Saying Goodbye to the Disciples: What Comes Next

SETTING UP THE STORY

We've read fifty-one stories of Jesus loving all kinds of people, showing us what God's love looks like and how we can extend God's love to others. There's so much we've learned about God's love that we can carry with us to bring unity and peace to our world! The disciples spent three years following in Jesus's footsteps. Now Jesus was about to leave them. The book of Acts begins with Jesus's final appearance to the disciples.

READ: ACTS 1:1–11 (NIV)

In my former book, Theophilus, I wrote about all that Jesus began to do and to teach until the day he was taken up to heaven, after giving instructions through the Holy Spirit to the apostles he had chosen. After his suffering, he presented himself to them and gave many convincing proofs that he was alive. He appeared to them over a period of forty days and spoke about the kingdom of God. On one occasion, while he was eating with them, he gave them this command: "Do not leave Jerusalem, but wait for the gift my Father promised, which you have heard me speak about. For John baptized with water, but in a few days you will be baptized with the Holy Spirit."

Then they gathered around him and asked him, "Lord, are you at this time going to restore the kingdom to Israel?"

He said to them: "It is not for you to know the times or dates the Father has set by his own authority. But you will receive power when the Holy Spirit comes on you; and you will be my witnesses in Jerusalem, and in all Judea and Samaria, and to the ends of the earth."

After he said this, he was taken up before their very eyes, and a cloud hid him from their sight.

They were looking intently up into the sky as he was going, when suddenly two men dressed in white stood beside them. "Men of Galilee," they said, "why do you stand here looking into the sky? This same Jesus, who has been taken from you into heaven, will come back in the same way you have seen him go into heaven."

TALK ABOUT IT

- How many days did Jesus appear to his disciples after he was raised from the dead?
- What did Jesus tell his disciples to wait for before they began teaching?
- What would the Holy Spirit give the disciples?
- What do you think it was like to be a disciple watching Jesus be "taken up" in the clouds?
- Is there anything that confuses you about this story? If so, it's okay! Let's talk about it.
- Do you have any questions about Acts 1:1–11?

CLOSING THOUGHT

Jesus spent his life showing people what it looked like to love others the way God loves us. After he died and rose again, his time on earth was short. He spent forty days after his resurrection reminding the disciples about all that he had taught them and called them to do. These were days of preparation. Jesus needed to prove that he had really risen from the dead. He needed to encourage the disciples to fulfill the mission: to go and make disciples of others, to show other people God's love and point them back to Jesus, the person through whom we can know God.

Through Jesus and his angels, God encouraged the disciples not to stand around staring up in the clouds waiting for Jesus to come back. Instead, it was time to get down to business loving others and spreading that message of truth and light to the world. So ends Jesus's ministry on earth and begins the ministry led by the Holy Spirit through the apostles, and then through thousands upon thousands of followers of Christ throughout the ages, all the way to today!

PRAYER PROMPT

God, thank you for revealing your true nature to us through your son Jesus Christ. Thank you for the promised gift of the Holy Spirit so that you are always with us. Thank you for the faithful writers who recorded your Son's life in these Gospels, for the faithful translators who have brought these stories to us in our language so that we can know you better through them. You are still working through your people every single day. Help us to be doers of your Word.

ACTIVITY #1: LETTER TO A FRIEND

The book of Acts is a letter addressed to a person named Theophilus. Write a letter to a family member or friend about something you've learned or experienced with God.

ACTIVITY #2: WRITE YOUR OWN BOOK OF ACTS

Keep a journal of the ways God is moving in your life. What opportunities has God given you to love others? What is God teaching you in your life? How has God proven himself faithful to you? What prayers has he answered? What verses are speaking to you?

Theophilus

The book of Acts is written by the same person who wrote the gospel of Luke. People aren't really sure who the actual person was who wrote these two books of the Bible, but we know the books were written to someone called Theophilus. His name comes from the Greek word *theophilos*, which means "friend of God."[4] It may have been an actual person, or it may have been an honorary title, like mister, miss, madam, or sir. Whether Theophilus was an actual person or the letter was addressing friends of God in general, the two books were written to an educated audience who were likely Roman and possibly not as well acquainted with Jewish Scripture.

Notes

GUIDE TO USING THIS DEVOTIONAL

1. "Latest Bible Translation Statistics," Wycliffe Bible Translators, October 2020, https://www.wycliffe.org.uk/about/our-impact/.
2. "Number of English Translations of the Bible," American Bible Society, December 2, 2009, https://news.americanbible.org /article/number-of-english-translations-of-the-bible.

SECTION 1: UNLIKELY DISCIPLES

1. "The Decapolis and Its Cities," Bible History Online, accessed April 28, 2021, https://www.bible-history.com/maps/decapolis _cities.html.
2. "The Meaning of Numbers: The Number 12," BibleStudy.org, accessed September 20, 2021, https://www.biblestudy.org /bibleref/meaning-of-numbers-in-bible/12.html.
3. Kenneth E. Bailey, "The Syro-Phoenician Woman," in *Jesus through Middle Eastern Eyes: Cultural Studies in the Gospels* (Downers Grove, IL: InterVarsity, 2008), 220–21.
4. Bailey, "The Syro-Phoenician Woman," 223.
5. Blue Letter Bible, s.v. "*pisteuō*," accessed April 28, 2021, https://www.blueletterbible.org/lang/Lexicon/Lexicon .cfm?strongs=G4100&t=KJV.
6. Blue Letter Bible, s.v. "*apistia*," accessed September 20, 2021, https://www.blueletterbible.org/lang/Lexicon/Lexicon .cfm?strongs=G570&t=KJV.
7. Kenneth E. Bailey, "The Woman in the House of Simon the Pharisee," in *Jesus through Middle Eastern Eyes: Cultural Studies in the Gospels* (Downers Grove, IL: InterVarsity, 2008), 239–60.
8. Bailey, "The Woman in the House of Simon the Pharisee," 242.
9. Bailey, "The Woman in the House of Simon the Pharisee," 243.

10. Bailey, "The Syro-Phoenician Woman," 220.

11. Kenneth E. Bailey, "Jesus and Women: An Introduction," in
    Jesus through Middle Eastern Eyes: Cultural Studies in the Gospels
    (Downers Grove, IL: InterVarsity, 2008), 193.

12. Kenneth E. Bailey, "The Blind Man and Zacchaeus," in *Jesus
    through Middle Eastern Eyes: Cultural Studies in the Gospels*
    (Downers Grove, IL: InterVarsity, 2008), 177–78.

13. Bailey, "The Blind Man and Zacchaeus," 178–81.

SECTION 2: THE DISCIPLES AND JESUS

1. Kenneth E. Bailey, "Jesus and Women: An Introduction," in
   Jesus through Middle Eastern Eyes: Cultural Studies in the Gospels
   (Downers Grove, IL: InterVarsity, 2008), 193.

2. W. D. Davies and Dale C. Allison Jr., *The Gospel According to
   Saint Matthew* (New York: T & T Clark, 1988), 1:600.

3. Kenneth E. Bailey, "The Parable of the Rich Fool," in *Jesus
   through Middle Eastern Eyes: Cultural Studies in the Gospels*
   (Downers Grove, IL: InterVarsity, 2008), 304.

4. Bailey, "The Blind Man and Zacchaeus," 172–73.

5. Genevieve Belmaker, "Jerusalem History: The First and Second
   Temples," Moon, accessed September 20, 2021, https://www
   .moon.com/travel/arts-culture/jerusalem-history-first-second
   -temples.

6. Belmaker, "Jerusalem History: The First and Second Temples."

7. Justo L. González, "Mission to the Gentiles," in *The Story of
   Christianity, Volume 1: The Early Church to the Dawn of the
   Reformation* (New York: Harper & Row, 1984), 29–30.

8. "The Acts of Philip," in *The New Testament Apocrypha*, ed. M. R.
   James (Berkeley, CA: Apocryphile Press, 2004), 439–53.

9. Blue Letter Bible, s.v. "*paraklētos*," accessed September 20, 2021,
   https://www.blueletterbible.org/lang/Lexicon/Lexicon
   .cfm?strongs=G3875&t=KJV.

10. Todd M. Johnson and Gina A. Zurlo, *World Christian Encyclopedia Online*, s.v. "Christian traditions," accessed April 28, 2021, http://dx.doi.org/10.1163/2666-6855_WCEO_COM_0405.

SECTION 3: PETER AND JESUS

1. *Encyclopedia Britannica*, s.v. "Gethsemane," July 20, 1998, https://www.britannica.com/place/Gethsemane.
2. See "oil of joy" in Psalm 45:7 and Isaiah 61:3 (NIV).
3. *Encyclopedia Britannica*, s.v. "Gethsemane."
4. Bible Hub, s.v. "*eimi*," accessed September 20, 2021, https://biblehub.com/greek/1510.htm.
5. Desmond Tutu and Mpho Tutu, *The Book of Forgiving: The Fourfold Path for Healing Ourselves and Our World* (New York: HarperOne, 2014).
6. "The Meaning of Numbers: The Number 3," BibleStudy.org, accessed September 20, 2021, https://www.biblestudy.org /bibleref/meaning-of-numbers-in-bible/3.html.

SECTION 4: IN THE FAMILY

1. Randy Ingermanson, "On the Road to Jerusalem with Jesus," May 10, 2019, https://www.ingermanson.com/blog/2019/05/10 /road-to-jerusalem-with-jesus/.
2. Jeannie Myers, "Who Was James, Jesus' Brother?" May 27, 2020, https://www.biblestudytools.com/bible-study/topical-studies /who-was-jesus-brother-james.html.
3. Blue Letter Bible, s.v. "strouthion," accessed September 20, 2021, https://www.blueletterbible.org/lang/Lexicon/Lexicon .cfm?strongs=G4765&t=KJV.
4. Herbert Lockyer, "Salome No. 2," originally published in *All the Women in the Bible* (Grand Rapids: Zondervan, 1988), https://www.biblegateway.com/resources/all-women-bible /Salome-No-2.

SECTION 5: LOVING OUR ENEMIES

1. Genelle Austin-Lett, "Temple Veil," BibleWise, accessed May 4, 2021, https://www.biblewise.com/bible_study/questions /temple-veil.php.

SECTION 6: THE DISCIPLES AND THE RESURRECTED LORD

1. Blue Letter Bible, s.v. "*pneuma,*" accessed September 20, 2021, https://www.blueletterbible.org/lang/lexicon/lexicon.cfm?Strongs =G4151&t=NIV.
2. Blue Letter Bible, s.v. "*phileō,*" accessed September 20, 2021, https://www.blueletterbible.org/lang/lexicon/lexicon.cfm?strongs =G5368.
3. Blue Letter Bible, s.v. "*agapē,*" accessed September 20, 2021, https://www.blueletterbible.org/lang/lexicon/lexicon.cfm ?strongs=G26.
4. Blue Letter Bible, s.v. "*theophilos,*" accessed September 20, 2021, https://www.blueletterbible.org/lang/lexicon/lexicon.cfm ?strongs=G2321.

About the Author

Sarah M. Wells loves to bring to life the stories God puts on her heart in whatever form they present themselves. In addition to *The Family Bible Devotionals*, she is also the author of a memoir *American Honey*, two collections of poems, a novel, and a pile of essays about faith, family, and the natural world. Sarah serves as a content writer for Root & Vine News, Spire Advertising, and Our Daily Bread Ministries' website, *God Hears Her*. She is a voracious reader, bird watcher, deck dweller, dog walker, chef and baker, joyful laugher, Brethren church member, champion introvert, and enjoyer of all God's creatures great and small. Sarah resides in Ashland, Ohio, with her husband, Brandon, and their three children—Lydia, Elvis, and Henry—and Izzy, their ever faithful Westie.

Web: sarahmariewells.com
🐦 @sarah_wells
f facebook.com/smwells1982
📷 instagram.com/sarahmwells1982/

Help us get the word out!

Our Daily Bread Publishing exists to feed the soul with the Word of God.

If you appreciated this book, please let others know.

- Pick up another copy to give as a gift.
- Share a link to the book or mention it on social media.
- Write a review on your blog, on a book-seller's website, or at our own site (odb.org/store).
- Recommend this book for your church, book club, or small group.

Connect with us:

f @ourdailybread

○ @ourdailybread

🐦 @ourdailybread

Our Daily Bread Publishing
PO Box 3566
Grand Rapids, Michigan 49501 USA

✉ books@odb.org